HOUSEPLANT CARE UNLOCKED

HOW ANYONE CAN ACHIEVE SUSTAINABLE &
THRIVING INDOOR PLANTS WITH STRESS-FREE
MAINTENANCE, PEST CONTROL, & MORE

NATALIA KOZLOVA

CONTENTS

1. THE JOY OF HOUSEPLANTS   5
   The Beauty and Bounty of Houseplants   7
   Setting the Stage for Stress-Free Plant Care   10

2. HOUSEPLANT BASICS   12
   The Fascinating World of Indoor Flora   13
   Choosing the Right Plants   14
   Setting up Your Indoor Garden   25
   Tools of the Trade   35

3. STRESS-FREE MAINTENANCE   39
   Maintenance Routines   41
   Troubleshooting Common Issues   45
   The Zen of Houseplant Care   47

4. PEST CONTROL AND MANAGEMENT   51
   Identifying Common Pests   52
   Natural Remedies and Prevention   59
   Chemical Options and When to Use Them   66

5. ADVANCED CARE TECHNIQUES   72
   Propagation and Pruning   73
   Mastering Indoor Plant Reproduction   86

6. ORCHID CARE DEMYSTIFIED   90
   Understanding Orchid Types   92
   Essential Orchid Care   98
   Orchid Troubleshooting and Maintenance   101

7. GREENING YOUR INDOOR SPACE   106
   Plant Placement and Styling   107
   Greening Difficult Spaces   113
   Themed Indoor Gardens   118

8. SUSTAINABILITY AND ECO-FRIENDLY
   HOUSEPLANT CARE   122
   Sustainable Gardening Practices   123
   Responsible Plant Acquisition   127
   Indoor Ecosystems   129

9. YOUR FLOURISHING INDOOR GARDEN   132
Creating a Personal Garden Sanctuary   133
Sharing the Love   135
Future Visions   138

BONUS CHAPTER: PET-FRIENDLY HOUSEPLANT
CARE   143
Identifying Toxic Houseplants   144
Poisonous Plant Alternatives   147
Managing Indoor Pet Behavior   148

References   151

1

THE JOY OF HOUSEPLANTS

I t was ten years ago when I grew my first plant, a beautiful shrub of vibrant red begonias. I had always been fascinated by plants even as a child, since we had our small backyard garden in my parents' home and our neighbors also grew a variety of flowering plants and vegetables. However, it would be some time before I got a chance to grow my own plants. For most of my twenties, I thought that I simply did not have the time nor the available space in my apartment to take up gardening. This all changed when a farmer's market opened up during the weekends nearby. One of the stores in the farmer's market sold beautiful flowers. Seeing the colorful plethora of flowers—tulips, orchids, carnations, peonies, and so much more—reminded me so much of my childhood neighborhood. As I went to buy an arrangement for my dining room, I noticed that the store also sold packets of flower seeds at the counter. On the drive back to my apartment, I began to consider planting one of those seeds and growing my own plant. "It would just be one houseplant," I thought, "and it would be fun to try growing something on my own." I did some research online to help me choose which flower to grow and settled on begonias. It was an annual plant, which meant that I would only be tending to the begonias for a season before they matured and bloomed. Even if I didn't succeed, I would have at least tried my hand at realizing a dream I've had since childhood. The next weekend, I bought the red begonia seeds at the farmer's market, along with a cute terracotta pot, a small pack of gardening soil, and a couple of basic gardening tools.

As I began growing my first houseplant, I continued expanding my knowledge of gardening, particularly gardening indoors. To be honest, this was the most demanding part of being a beginner gardener. I tried to learn everything I could about the specific needs of my begonia, as well as foundational gardening practices. The actual tending to my houseplant was surprisingly easy, and, more importantly, fun. It became a pleasurable part of my day to water my begonia, and even just watching it grow gave me time for relaxation from my busy schedule. By the late summer of that year, my begonias were in full bloom. I had succeeded in growing my first houseplant! I felt immense satisfaction and accomplishment seeing the wonderful, bright red flowers adorning my apartment patio. From then on, I was hooked. I eagerly sought to grow more plants in the subsequent seasons, all while continuing to learn more about indoor gardening. All the while, I made it my priority to keep gardening convenient and stress-free, discovering and adopting practices that made the hobby fit my lifestyle and my needs. My indoor gardening journey was not always easy nor successful, however. I remember my first attempt at growing plants in winter went unfavorably, as my apartment did not receive much sunlight during this season. However, these challenges only made me more experienced in growing houseplants, as I understood first-hand what factors I needed to consider when tending to plants indoors. It is this knowledge and experience in growing houseplants that I want to share with you so that like me, you too can have the incomparable joy of gardening.

The Beauty and Bounty of Houseplants

Plants and human beings have an intimate and deep relationship that they have shared for thousands of years. It is plant life on this planet that provides the oxygen necessary for animals like us human beings to survive and thrive. Of course, plants are a major food source for humans—all of the staple foods around the world like bread and rice are gifts from our green companions. In Michael Pollan's book The Omnivore's Dilemma (2006), which traces the history of food, he notes how archaeologists attribute the founding of human civilizations to the domestication of plant species like wheat and corn. In short, we owe the societies we live in today to plants. As the threat of anthropogenic climate change looms in the immediate future, recognizing the importance of our relationship with plants becomes even more important. Adopting sustainability practices and protecting the ecologies that sustain plant life around the world are endeavors we need to seriously and meaningfully pursue.

Our relationship with plants goes beyond the provision of our basic needs like oxygen and food. Being in environments teeming with plant life is, in many ways, our natural condition. This is proven by the many studies showing how having greenery in our surroundings has a significant positive impact on human beings' mental health. For example, the recent study conducted by Dzhambov, et al. (2021) investigated whether the presence of plants in indoor and outdoor surroundings mitigated the adverse mental health effects of quarantine during the 2020 COVID-19 pandemic. The results of the research showed that individuals whose surroundings had greenery present during quarantine experienced reduced symptoms of anxiety and depression, as well as lower rates of clinically-meaningful depression and anxiety levels (Dzhambov, et al., 2021). The presence of indoor plants was especially effective in helping quarantined people to cope with being away from their families. It is no surprise that many celebrities also took up indoor gardening during the pandemic. Breaking Bad actor Aaron Paul, Santa Clarita Diet star Drew Barrymore, and the musician couple Blake Shelton and Gwen Stefani all started growing houseplants as a relaxing and calming hobby during such a stressful time (Hansen, 2020). In many ways, our green friends not only nourish the physical needs of our bodies, but they also nourish our minds.

Growing indoor plants can also be a very practical hobby for anyone concerned with living a healthier lifestyle or becoming self-sustaining. It is more than feasible to grow herbs, vegetables, and even some fruits indoors, depending on the available space or the amount of investment in equipment you are willing to commit. Growing basil, cilantro, or parsley in your kitchen is easy and requires little to no maintenance. If you've ever seen TV shows where celebrity chefs like Jamie Oliver and Gordon Ramsey cook in their home kitchens, you'll notice how they have small pots of herbs adorning their countertops or dining tables (Avery, 2022). Fresh herbs are, after all, more flavorful, which means growing them indoors will elevate your cooking. If you live in a particularly sunny area, several varieties of lettuce and peppers are suitable to grow indoors. There are also relatively inexpensive starter kits for setting up your indoor hydroponics system—this is a setup that allows the growing of plants without soil. Many commercially available hydroponics starter kits have a very small footprint, and you can grow microgreens that are the perfect ingredients for healthy salads. Citrus fruits like lemons, oranges, and clementines have several varieties that are suitable for growing indoors. Not only can you enjoy fresh fruits grown in your own home, but the bright colors of indoor fruit plants also make them wonderful ornamental plants. Besides the convenience of fruit and vegetables being readily available for you and your family to enjoy, the fact that you've grown these crops yourself also means that you can be sure that they are healthy and safe, without the dangerous chemicals and additives that often come with industrially-grown produce.

Finally, let us recognize and appreciate how plants are beautiful, lush, and living things. Houseplants come in a wide variety of shapes, sizes, colors, and visual textures, so you will have plenty of choices for decorating your home, no matter the architectural design or aesthetic style. Ornamental plants like philodendrons and pothos are great in Modernist apartments, as they fit the minimalist aesthetic while still giving life to your indoor spaces. Flowering annuals that thrive in shade like fuchsias, impatiens, and lobelias impart splashes of color to enliven more rustic homes. Crawling vines like Boston ferns, live ivy, and string of pearls can be grown in "living walls" that can adorn bare walls, showcasing the greenery like works of art. Even if you live in a hotter, drier climate than in temperate areas, you can grow succulents and cacti to match the surroundings. As with art, you can express yourself through the beauty of the houseplants you choose to grow. You might have a very eclectic, eccentric sense of personal style, which can manifest in an indoor garden composed of gorgeous, exotic plants from around the world. Or you might be a very pragmatic and utilitarian person, who finds expression in tending to a hardy ornamental shrub in your living room or a spartan container vegetable garden on your patio. Indoor plants are not just pretty ornaments that decorate your home—they become reflections of your personality.

Setting the Stage for Stress-Free Plant Care

Like me ten years ago, your idea of growing plants might be creating your own backyard garden. This iconic image of gardening can be intimidating, especially if you consider the time, labor, and investment you think you'll have to commit to such an endeavor. In this context, gardening might seem like a difficult and stressful hobby. When it comes to starting out, the idealized image of a back-yard garden is a misconception. Starting small is always an option —like me, you might begin your gardening journey with a single houseplant that you grow in a season. Testing out your green thumb is a great way to gain valuable gardening experience. You will discover what aspects of plant care work for you, and assess the unique environmental conditions in your home. You'll find that much of the effort in indoor gardening is front-loaded at the beginning. Yes, there are many crucial decisions to make in determining which houseplants you'll be growing, where in your house or apartment you'll situate your garden, and identifying how to satisfy the needs of your houseplants. But once you've made these decisions, the actual tending to your plants requires minimal effort, and the routines you'll develop will end up being relaxing experiences that you look forward to every day.

Historian and avid gardener Alice Morse Earle once said, "Half the interest of a garden is the constant exercise of the imagination" (2014). Gardening is a creative and imaginative hobby, and you have many opportunities to grow houseplants without having to deal with the stress and anxieties that come with tending to many plants in an outdoor garden. Indeed, a large part of the joy of indoor gardening is exploring fresh, new ways that you can make plants a part of your life. The knowledge I want to share with you in this book aims to inspire this creative process. I want to provide you with many options that allow you to choose how you approach the hobby: Plant care techniques and setups that can be used what ever your space requirements or daily schedule might be, methods of propagation that suit your gardening skill level and your available resources, and sustainable gardening essentials that accommodate your lifestyle. By the end of the book, I hope that all the knowledge you've gained will grant you the confidence to pursue any path you like in your indoor gardening journey.

2

HOUSEPLANT BASICS

The Fascinating World of Indoor Flora

Human beings have been growing plants indoors for a very long time. The ancient Egyptians brought palm trees and lotus flowers inside their homes, and are credited for inventing the clay pot, the ubiquitous plant-growing container still popularly used today (Abdalla, 2023). The Hanging Gardens of Babylon, one of the seven wonders of the ancient world, was renowned for growing a marvelous variety of plant life in an artificially constructed space. The Romans and their massive villas featured indoor ornamental plants from throughout the empire. The great Roman statesman and philosopher Marcus Tullius Cicero once said, "If you have a garden and a library, you have everything you need." In the Western world, indoor gardening saw a rise in popularity during the seventeenth century, as European explorers and colonists discovered new types of flora all around the world (Lusiardi, 2023). The exotic beauty and appeal of plants from the New World and the Orient became a status symbol in countries like Britain, France, and Spain, resulting in the desire for people to showcase these new plants in their homes. The Victorian era in the nineteenth century saw another surge in the popularity of growing houseplants, particularly with the emergence of the artistic and cultural movement known as Art Nouveau. Art Nouveau saw beauty in organic, natural forms—floral patterns and plant motifs became prolific in art and architecture during this time (Kleiner, 2020). As such, incorporating plant life into architectural designs was widely adopted in the Victorian era. The Modernist architecture of the twentieth century had a similar aesthetic ideal, wanting to integrate both natural and urban spaces into a cohesive whole. Today, indoor gardening also finds a practical purpose, as households wanting to achieve self-sufficiency and grow their own herbs, fruits, and vegetables indoors.

This brief history of indoor gardening demonstrates the inherent fascination of humans with plants. Even as our societies and cultures become more civilized, we still long to maintain our intimate relationship with nature. Our fascination with plants is, in some ways, surprising since plants are organisms that are vastly different from us. They "breathe" carbon dioxide while we breathe oxygen, produce their food through the miraculous process of photosynthesis when we cannot, and many plants like the giant redwood trees can live for hundreds of years, many times longer than a human lifetime. Ultimately, however, plants are still living things, which is why we maintain a natural connection with them. Like all living things, plants thrive when we give them attention, affection, and love. To accomplish this while ensuring that our gardening experience remains stress-free, we will need to establish a strong foundation of basic plant care practices.

Choosing the Right Plants

One of the most significant decisions you will have to make as an indoor gardener is deciding on the plants you want to grow. This can be an overwhelming task, as you have thousands of species and tens of thousands of varieties to choose from—even just finding a good starting point can already be challenging by itself. We will be discussing the various factors you have to consider in making your decision, but my recommendation is to choose a plant that naturally grows in your local region. Growing a plant from the local habitat has several advantages that make caring for it easy and stress-free.

For beginner indoor gardeners, growing local plants makes your first foray into the hobby easier because:

- Local plants are already well-suited to the environmental conditions of your home. There is no need for special equipment to maintain ideal lighting, temperature, or humidity.
- Resources like fertilizer and gardening soil are cheaper and more readily available. You won't have to import more specialized resources that plants exotic to your region might need.
- It is easier to grow local plants in sustainable and environmentally-conscious ways. They are resistant to your region's diseases and pests, resulting in less use of chemical pesticides.

For more experienced indoor gardeners, local plants offer interesting challenges and opportunities:

- You can create a closed ecosystem indoors using local plants. You will essentially have a botanical showroom in your home that features a balanced mix of flora that complement each other functionally and aesthetically.
- Local plants make growing crops with high yields possible even in an indoor environment. The ready availability of resources allows you to significantly scale up your production of vegetables.
- You can aid in the recovery of local endangered plant species. Growing threatened local species indoors allows you to contribute to the rejuvenation of ecosystems in your area.

There are many places where you can get more information that will aid you in deciding which houseplants will best fit your life-style. You can conduct research online, finding websites or YouTube channels of gardeners who also live in your region. A source of knowledge that is often overlooked by those new to the hobby is the gardening stores, plant nurseries, and greenhouses in your locale. Small gardening supply stores are usually owned by experienced gardeners, so feel free to talk to them and ask them which local flora that are prolific in your area would make for good houseplants. Plant nurseries and greenhouses grow seedlings for sale to gardeners, hobbyists, and farmers. As such, many have horti-culturists and botanists working in these businesses, who will happily share valuable information about local plant life with you. Finally, many states and countries have branches of government agricultural departments. You can consult with them online or in person regarding recommendations for houseplants that grow best in your area. They have especially useful information if you want to grow crops in your indoor garden. Many have state programs that encourage people to grow their own food. As such, they may even provide you with seeds, seedlings, and other materials necessary to set up your indoor garden.

Assessing Your Space and Needs

You'll find that even after limiting your options to local species for your indoor garden, there will still be many options to choose from when it comes to growing your first houseplants. Your next major consideration in choosing what plants to grow will be based on your personal wants and needs. Ask yourself the crucial question: "Why am I growing houseplants?" Your purpose for indoor gardening will be of great help in making your choice of plants to grow. Are you growing houseplants to beautify your home? Then annuals that produce brightly colored flowers like zinnias, lobelias, or nasturtiums are what you want. Do you want your indoor garden to provide a calming and relaxing atmosphere? Fragrant flora like eucalyptus, lavender, and jasmine are your best bets. Are you planning to grow herbs and vegetables to have fresh ingredients in your dishes? Mint, oregano, scallions, and radishes all thrive indoors, and there are even varieties of tomatoes and spinach that require less exposure to light than their traditional, outdoor counterparts. I highly recommend that you make a list of the things you want to get out of your indoor garden. Write this list down on a piece of paper or save it on your phone, so that you can bring it with you when you peruse potential seeds and plants at your local gardening store or plant nursery. This way, you can ask for recommendations that best fulfill your needs.

A more practical restriction to your houseplant choices will be the available space you have in your home. Gardening indoors already imposes some spatial limitations—you can't grow a full grove of apple trees in your living room, after all. Your indoor garden will also need access to plenty of natural light, which may make the viable space even smaller. That said, the problem of having a smaller space in your home for houseplants can be overcome, albeit with additional costs for space-saving containers, tools, and setups. One such setup uses hydroponics, where plants are grown indoors by immersing them in a water/nutrient solution. The Deep Water Culture (DWC) system is the most popular hydroponics setup among gardeners today (Grant, 2022). Complete DWC kits can be quite expensive, and even though you can construct and install a DWC setup by yourself, this requires a lot of technical knowledge while still incurring significant costs for the necessary equipment. Still, if you are willing to invest, having a hydroponics setup for your indoor garden will save a lot of space and will reduce the maintenance in growing your plants. More traditional ways to maximize the available space for your plants include choosing space-efficient plant containers such as hanging plant boxes and pots or growing plants that flourish in smaller containers, like begonias and yuccas.

Low-Maintenance vs. High-Maintenance Plants

Different plants require differing levels of care and attention in order to grow to their fullest. As such, the amount of maintenance a plant requires will certainly impact houseplant decisions. Most people would prefer to grow "low-maintenance" indoor plants like the snake plant, the money plant, or the Kentia palm. These species do not need to be watered and fertilized often, can grow even in low-light conditions, and are hardy enough to flourish in very hot or very cold climates. The convenience of low-maintenance plants is certainly very appealing, but they do have aspects that may not make them right for you. Low-maintenance plants are, to put it bluntly, quite plain and unexciting. Low-maintenance species do not produce flowers nor fruits, and while some offer interesting visual textures, they won't draw the attention of your guests. Very few low-maintenance plants are edible, consisting mainly of herbs that still require ideal environmental conditions. In short, low-maintenance plants are not very engaging from a gardener's perspective. You are likely to find yourself getting bored tending to these flora, and soon you might lose interest in the hobby altogether.

High-maintenance plants are more demanding species to work with, often having unique and exacting requirements for them to even just survive. These kinds of plants will vary in their water, lighting, and nutritional needs depending on the season and their stage of life. Roses, for example, are notorious for being high-maintenance plants—they need constant watering, fertilizing, and pruning, their needs changing from when the rose is still a seedling to when they start flowering. Despite the significant attention that high-maintenance plants require, many gardeners prefer them to low-maintenance plants. It's not just because experienced gardeners want the challenge of successfully growing these difficult flora. All your flowering and fruiting annuals will be high-maintenance plants, which means that the "stars" of your indoor garden will always be the plants that require more attention and care. What this means is that if you want beautiful and colorful flowers like anthuriums or chrysanthemums adorning your living room, or you want to have fresh lettuce or even tomatoes in your dishes, then you will have to grow high-maintenance plants. Don't be daunted by the effort and investment these plants require, as successfully growing them is one of the great pleasures of indoor gardening.

Unique Houseplants to Consider

There are many common and dependable plant species familiar to gardeners around the world; these are your anthuriums and begonias, Chinese money trees, and rubber plants that are hardy and easy to grow indoors, while still having interesting colors and visual textures to beautify indoor spaces. But perhaps in deciding which plants you want in your home, you prefer the more out-of-the-ordinary options. Here are five unique species and varieties that will make your indoor garden stand out.

Fittonia/Nerve Plant – This flowering perennial immediately catches your attention with its visually striking foliage. The fittonia's dark green, oval leaves contrast sharply with white or bright red veins. As a tropical plant, the fittonia is a high-maintenance plant, requiring high humidity and plenty of sunlight. The effort is definitely worth it to have this unique houseplant in your home.

Dwarf Pineapple – The dwarf pineapple, scientific name Ananas comosus, is one of the most impressive houseplants you can grow. It produces a single, ornamental pineapple fruit on top of a lush foliage of leaves. The dwarf pineapple will make for a wonderful botanical centerpiece in your living room or dedicated indoor garden. It is also a surprisingly hardy plant, with regular watering being its only main requirement. Note that dwarf pineapples are in quite high demand, so make sure to grab any opportunity to buy one when they become available.

The Dancing Plant/Telegraph Plant – This tropical shrub is one of the most unique plant species, as it responds to lights and sounds by moving its smaller leaflets, hence its name. The slow, mesmerizing movements of the dancing plant's leaves will delight your family, friends, and guests. Note that the dancing plant requires plenty of light, which you may need to supplement with artificial lighting.

Dolphin Succulents – Relatively few gardeners opt to grow succulents, which is a shame since most succulents are low maintenance while still being aesthetically interesting. The dolphin succulent gets its name from its fleshy leaves that are shaped like dolphins. It does not need a lot of sunlight to thrive and is hardy enough to grow successfully in a wide range of temperatures.

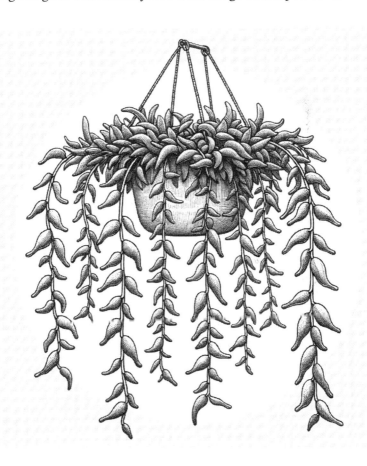

Miniature Brown Turkey Fig Tree – Miniature trees are fantastic options for growing fruits indoors. Miniature lemons and limes are quite popular among indoor gardeners, but if you want something different, consider getting a Brown Turkey fig tree. It produces a sizeable yield of figs that you can use in many Mediterranean and Middle Eastern recipes. Fig trees, like all fruiting plants, require lots of sunlight. Be careful of overwatering them, however, to avoid root rot.

Setting up Your Indoor Garden

Once you've decided on the houseplants you want to grow, the next step is to prepare all of the necessities for our green friends. This stage is crucial to the success of your indoor garden, as the very survival of your houseplants depends on how well you can provide for their basic needs. Mistakes during this time will only have their consequences made apparent weeks, if not months later. Your plant box might be too small to accommodate the sprawling root system of your rubber plant. Failing to provide insufficient direct sunlight to your geraniums will leave them stunted and unable to flower in the summer season. The inability to maintain high humidity levels where you are growing your majestic parlor palm may even result in the plant drying out and dying. You can't easily change the conditions you've created for your houseplants once they start growing, which only emphasizes how crucial it is that you set up your indoor garden correctly. The key to success in this stage is careful planning. Creating a checklist that contains all of your houseplants' basic needs will be invaluable so that you don't miss anything when preparing your setup. Identifying growth milestones for your plants is also useful. Knowing the average size of the plant and key characteristics in each stage of its development will help you monitor the health of your flora. Furthermore, this will make planning for the conditions when the plant is fully grown easier. As we go over the primary considerations for your houseplants' basic needs, take note of how they apply to the species you have chosen to grow. All plants may have the same necessities, but each single houseplant will be unique and will require varying amounts of these necessities.

The Perfect Containers and Soil

There are three main considerations when choosing the right containers for your houseplants: size, drainage, and material. Your containers need to be the right size so that your plants have the right amount of room to grow. If the container is too small, your houseplants might grow stunted, as their root systems become too crowded and they are unable to absorb enough water and nutrients from the soil. Planning is essential when choosing the right container size for your plants. If you are starting with a seedling or young plant, choose a pot that has a diameter that is about two inches larger than the current size of the plant. This should give it enough space as the plant continues to grow. If you are starting with seeds, most seed packets will identify the maximum size of the variety, so choose the appropriate container for when the plant matures. In terms of the depth of the container, providing six inches of soil depth should be enough space for indoor plants to comfortably grow. Note that vegetables, even "shallow-rooting" varieties of lettuce and spinach, will need more soil depth—if you are planning to grow vegetables indoors, you will need containers at least 12 inches deep.

Proper drainage is another important consideration when choosing your plant containers. There needs to be a way for excess water to drain out of a plant box or pot because this water will impede your houseplants' root respiration. Air pockets will form naturally in the soil where your plant is growing, and your plant's roots will absorb the oxygen that becomes trapped there to carry out important botanical processes. Excess water will fill up these air pockets, essentially suffocating your plants. Most commercially available plant containers have holes or slits at the bottom to allow for proper drainage. If you are constructing your containers, however, make sure to include these drainage openings to keep your houseplants healthy. Also note that because all plant containers will need drainage, you will need a way to collect this excess water and prevent it from spilling in your indoor spaces. For most cases, placing a saucer or bowl beneath your plant containers should do the job, but remember to discard the excess water once the saucer is full. There are also dedicated plant drainage trays that are commercially available, and many provide attachments for hoses to channel the excess water away for disposal, preventing damage to your floor and furnishings.

The material of your plant containers matters a great deal. You can of course choose containers based on whether their "look" fits the style of the indoor space—wood containers look great in rustic settings, while metal containers fit the minimalist aesthetic very well. That said, the material of your plant containers also impacts thermal conditions and water retention in the soil. Below are common plant container materials and their advantages and disadvantages when it comes to meeting your and your plants' needs.

Wood Planters

+ Advantages: a good insulating capacity that protects your plants from extremely high or extremely low temperatures, is lightweight, and allows for portability.

— Disadvantages: low durability, and even treated wood will eventually degrade and rot.

Clay/Terracotta Containers

+ Advantages: very porous material that allows excess water to evaporate and the soil to be aerated for root respiration, high thermal mass that absorbs and stores heat effectively, making temperature regulation easy.

— Disadvantages: tends to flake and crack in colder temperatures without adequate protection, fairly heavy material that limits portability.

Sheet Metal Containers

✚ Advantages: very durable while remaining lightweight, allowing for portability, easy to construct on your own.

— Disadvantages: highly conductive material, making temperature control difficult.

Plastic and Resin Containers

✚ Advantages: fairly durable, lightweight, and very cheap, comes in many varieties to fit various styles.

— Disadvantages: non-porous material that prevents soil aeration, and does not allow for water drainage without proper drainage holes.

In the world of gardening, "soil" is a technical term that refers to a growth medium comprised of inorganic (rocks and minerals) and organic (decaying animal and plant matter) materials. This mixture is ideal for growing plants because the inorganic components provide the soil with the structural characteristics that plants need —such as aeration and root anchorage—while the organic materials both contain essential plant nutrients and retain the nutrients of additional fertilizer for absorption by the roots. Using a growth medium that is made up exclusively of inorganic components is not preferable, since materials like clay or sand are chemically inert, which means that even if you constantly add fertilizers to the medium, they will not be retained for absorption. It is possible to use a purely organic growth medium; compost is made up entirely of decayed plant and animal matter and is commonly used in gardening. However, the biological processes in decaying tend to raise the pH levels of such growth media, resulting in very acidic growth conditions that are detrimental to many plant species and varieties. This is why even gardeners who use homemade compost often add inorganic materials such as limestone to reduce acidity. Most of the commercially available "garden soil" already offers the ideal mix of inorganic and organic material for temperate zone plants, and should be a solid option as the soil for your houseplants. That said, some of the varieties you might choose to grow may have special soil needs. You can examine the back of the packages of commercial garden soil to view the ingredients and their corresponding ratios. Here are some of the most common commercial garden soil ingredients and how they affect your plants. This information should help you decide which garden soil will work best for your houseplants.

Perlite and Pumice

Perlite and pumice are both inorganic materials that allow plenty of aeration and water drainage in the garden soil. Pumice is slightly heavier and more expensive than perlite, which is why you will find more garden soil using perlite than pumice. Garden soil with high ratios of perlite or pumice is great for plants that are sensitive to overwatering.

Vermiculite

Vermiculite is a mineral composed mainly of clay particles. As such, this garden soil ingredient allows for greater water retention capacity. Garden soil that contains a lot of vermiculite is perfect for many tropical plants that need constant moisture.

Zeolite

Zeolite is an inorganic material that combines the benefits of perlite, pumice, and vermiculite. It is porous enough in structure to allow aeration for root respiration, but can also retain up to 60% of its weight in water. Zeolite's water retention does not impede root respiration and allows the plant to draw moisture from the soil when it needs it. The only disadvantage of garden soil that uses zeolite is that it will be more expensive, given the rarity of this ingredient.

Peat

Peat or peat moss is a special kind of compost comprised of decayed plant and animal matter only found in marshy areas called bogs or moors. Peat is a highly sought-after inorganic material in garden soils, as it absorbs and retains nutrients exceedingly well. A problem with choosing garden soil that uses peat as an ingredient is that harvesting peat is damaging to the environment. When peat is extracted from bogs, large amounts of carbon dioxide are released into the atmosphere.

Coco Coir

Coco coir is an inorganic garden soil ingredient composed of decayed, shredded coconut husks. Coconut husks are natural byproducts of the coconut industry, as they are the fibers that make up the discarded shells of coconuts when processed for food production. Coco coir is currently the most popular, sustainable alternative to peat. Coco coir is still not as good at absorbing and retaining nutrients as peat moss, but it comes close.

Proper Lighting and Temperature

All plants require a source of light to survive. Your green companions draw energy from light to conduct photosynthesis, transforming molecules and elements from the soil and carbon dioxide into their food. In nature, plants rely on the sun as their main light source. One of the main challenges of growing plants indoors is maintaining access to natural sunlight, as the rooms of your home will not always receive enough illumination to sustain your houseplants. Plants don't all have the same light needs; therefore, you must know just the ideal lighting conditions that would lead to your plants thriving indoors. Among gardeners, the terms "sun" and "shade" are used to describe the different light requirements among plants. Plant nurseries and greenhouses will indicate the amounts of sun or shade a seedling needs, and seed packets will also utilize these terms to provide buyers with information to plan for ideal lighting conditions. The four light requirement terms used in gardening are:

Full Sun – 6 to 8 hours of exposure to direct sunlight daily during the summer season.

Partial Sun – 3 to 4 hours of exposure to direct sunlight daily during the summer season.

Partial Shade – 2 hours of exposure to direct sunlight; or 12 hours in a shaded area daily during the summer season.

Full Shade – half an hour or less exposure to direct sunlight daily throughout the year.

Houseplants that require direct exposure to sunlight will have to be placed near windows, glass doors, and/or skylights. Those that require indirect sunlight can be placed in the same indoor spaces with plenty of access to natural light, but in places where they are not directly exposed to the sun's rays. If you are planning to rely on natural light to meet your houseplants' lighting needs, it would be very useful to keep track of sunlight availability in your home. Fortunately, there are many available phone apps like Sun Surveyor, Sun Locator Lite, and Sun Seeker that you can download for free to help you track sunlight throughout the day. Once you know how much natural light the various areas of your home receive, it should be easy to plan where to locate your houseplants and indoor garden.

If you live in a region where sunlight is only available for a few hours in a day, or you want to grow your houseplants in a space within your home without much access to natural light, then relying on artificial lights is a viable option. In contemporary gardening, full-spectrum, LED growing lights are the most popularly used, as they are relatively cheap, easy to set up, and flexible because they are modular (Leone, 2017). For most houseplants, you want to use full-spectrum LED growing lights with an output of 20 lumens per watt, as this simulates sunlight most closely. There are LED growing light kits that are ready to install and use immediately, although you can also opt to create your own setup by buying individual LED growing light diodes. There are also specialized growing lights available in gardening supply stores that output more of a particular light wavelength to meet the lighting needs of more exotic species and varieties. An ideal growing light setup has the LED lights installed 6 to 12 inches away from the topmost part of a houseplant's foliage—this counts as "direct sunlight" for most plant species. For plants that need indirect sunlight, you can just lower the luminosity of the LED lights to half. Keep the growing lights on depending on the sun or shade requirements, and there are automated LED growing kits available that allow you to set the number of hours of exposure for your houseplants.

Maintaining the ideal temperature for your indoor garden can be challenging, particularly if you are growing plant varieties not native to your region. If you don't plan on using temperature control systems in your indoor garden, then it is best that you choose plants that can thrive in your climate region. For those living in the continental United States, you can consult the free, interactive US Department of Agriculture Plant Hardiness Zone Map available on the USDA website. The USDA Plant Hardiness Zone Map assigns a code to each climate region in the continental US. Seed packets will identify in which regions that particular plant can grow given the local temperature range. Once you've identified which region you belong to, you can select the appropriate house-plants for your indoor garden. Many countries have similar Hardiness Zone Maps available on the websites of their respective agricultural departments. High temperatures are typically the ideal thermal conditions for plants, and maintaining such conditions will go hand in hand with the humidity levels of your indoor garden. We will be discussing humidity and the equipment you can use to keep temperature and humidity levels at a certain amount in the next subsection.

Humidity and Watering Essentials

Humidity refers to the amount of water vapor present in the air. While the ideal level of humidity varies depending on the species, in general, plants require relatively high humidity levels to remain healthy and productive. This is because humidity influences the respiration of plants. Plants "breathe" through small openings on the underside of their leaves called stomata. During respiration, the stomata open to let in carbon dioxide and expel oxygen. However, a consequence of the open stomata is that they provide a means for water to evaporate. The plant essentially risks losing precious water every time it opens its stomata. Evaporation is especially likely to occur in dry, low-humidity environments. Thus, many plant species will close their stomata when their surroundings have little moisture in the air (Chia & Lim, 2022). This in turn prevents efficient respiration, which is detrimental to the plant's health. This is why —with the exception of succulents and hardier varieties—many plants will need to be situated in humid environments. The best way to maintain the ideal humidity conditions for your plants is to use a humidifier. Even the cheaper ones should be sufficient to meet your greenery's needs, though more expensive humidifiers specially designed for houseplants will allow you to set precise moisture levels for your indoor garden. A more "low-tech" option is to make your own humidity tray, which just involves filling a tray with water and placing your pots or plant boxes on top. You may want to add pebbles or small rocks to the humidity tray, just so the bottoms of your plant containers are not submerged in water and prevent overwatering your houseplants.

Speaking of watering your houseplants, you also have many choices when it comes to meeting your indoor garden's watering requirements. A basic watering can is enough for many situations, especially if you are only tending to a few houseplants in your home. You won't need to constantly water your plants; in fact, many gardeners make the mistake of overwatering, drowning the soil and hampering root respiration. We'll discuss scheduling when to water your plants in the next chapter, but for now, what is important is that you recognize that making sure that your plant's water needs are being met is not as demanding as you might think. If you have a larger indoor garden with several dozen plants in your collection, manual watering can become a significant inconvenience. If this is the situation in your home, then you may want to invest in installing or constructing an automated watering system. There are many options you can go for: automatic sprinklers that activate at specific times of the day, drip watering systems that release water at calibrated intervals, and even variants that can be controlled through a phone app. All automated watering systems will need some access to a water source, most likely via your home's indoor plumbing. Providing such access can greatly add to the cost depending on where your indoor garden is located.

Tools of the Trade

When you visit your local gardening supplies shop or home improvement store, you will see hundreds of gardening-related products promising to make tending to and caring for your plants easy and effective. No doubt, many of these products will indeed make indoor gardening a more convenient experience for you. However, most of these products are just nice-to-haves, not must-haves in caring for your houseplants. You only need a few essential gardening tools at hand to be successful in indoor gardening: a pair of gardening gloves, a hand fork, a hand trowel, a pair of pruning shears, and a watering can. With these five tools, you should be able to provide your houseplants with all the care and attention that they need while keeping gardening an easy, stress-free experience.

Gardening Gloves

Gardening gloves keep your hands clean and protect you from cuts and scrapes when doing your gardening tasks. The ideal gardening gloves strike a balance between durability and comfort—you want a pair that is durable enough in construction while not being too bulky to hamper your dexterity when doing delicate work. Cotton and leather are traditional materials for garden gloves, though only leather is naturally water-resistant. Gardening gloves can also be made of newer fabrics that are water-resistant and durable, while still being lightweight and breathable to be worn comfortably for long periods.

Hand Fork

A hand fork is a versatile tool in indoor gardening. It is a smaller, handheld version of a rake. Indeed, hand forks have the same function of tilling and aerating the soil to both make the soil easier to work with and to encourage good root respiration. When choosing a hand fork that is right for you, prioritize how comfortable it is to work with the tool. In this regard, a lightweight, stainless steel hand fork would be ideal, as it makes using the hand fork easier while still being resistant to rust.

Hand Trowel

The hand trowel is the iconic indoor gardener's tool. It is used to transfer soil between houseplant containers, dig holes for bulbs or transplanting seedlings, and removing weeds that may grow in your indoor garden. Like the hand fork, the hand trowel is a miniature version of an outdoor gardening tool, the shovel. Hand trowels can come in different shapes for specialized functions such as transplanting, or digging through hard, dry soil.

Pruning Shears

Pruning is an important aspect of houseplant care, as it encourages growth in your plants while keeping their foliage manageable in indoor spaces. Bypass pruners are the best type of pruning shears for use in your indoor garden, as they make cleaner cuts than anvil-type pruners. If you have reduced hand strength or suffer from arthritis, you may want to get a ratchet pruner, as it requires less force to use effectively. Always keep your pruning shears sharp, not only to make pruning easier but also to maintain clean cuts to the stems and leaves of your houseplants.

Watering Can

If you are not using an automated watering system, the simple watering can will be responsible for meeting your houseplants' watering needs. As with most indoor gardening tools, you want to choose your watering can based on comfort—the amount of water it can hold should be just enough that you can easily hold and carry the vessel. A watering can with a long, sturdy handle should support the water container's weight while still making tilting and pouring easy. A good indoor watering can has a long, narrow spout since you want to water the soil in the container without having to lean forwards too much. A narrow spout also makes it easy to avoid watering your houseplants' leaves and foliage. Water droplets left on the leaves of your plants can lead to leaf scorching, especially if the plant is exposed to direct sunlight.

Fertilizers and Supplements

Most people conceive of fertilizers as "artificial additives" that promote faster growth in plants. In truth, fertilizers are crucial in meeting the nutritional needs of all plants. As we discussed earlier, the organic matter in soil provides your plants with nutrients, but these nutrients will eventually run out as the plant absorbs them over time or they wash away during watering. In the wild, the soil is able to replenish its nutrients when decaying organic matter like the carcasses of animals or dead branches and leaves breaks down and mixes with the ground soil. Fertilizing your houseplants simply replaces this natural process so that your plants still get the nutrients they need to survive and thrive. If you are already composting in your home, you have a plentiful supply of natural fertilizer for your houseplants. Otherwise, you will likely need to buy commercial fertilizers available in gardening supplies and home improvement stores. The most important thing you need to know when buying commercial fertilizers is the N-P-K percentages indicated in the fertilizers' packaging. These refer to the percentage of each of the three essential macronutrients—nitrogen (N), phosphorous (P), and potassium (K)—in that specific fertilizer. For example, a fertilizer with N-P-K percentages at 17-18-28 will have 1.7 lbs. of nitrogen, 1.8 lbs. of phosphorous, and 2.8 lbs. of potassium for every 10 lbs. of that particular fertilizer. Different plant species may need higher proportions of these three macronutrients, so choose the ideal fertilizer accordingly. Supplements typically provide your plants with secondary macronutrients and micronutrients, like sulfur, calcium, copper, and iron. They are mostly necessary when growing rare and exotic houseplants. You can usually find the nutritional requirements of a particular plant on many reputable brands of seed packets, or you can consult with your local greenhouse or plant nursery.

3

STRESS-FREE MAINTENANCE

The world-renowned landscape artist and garden designer Geoffrey Jellicoe recognized the rejuvenating power of gardens: "The charm of the garden lies in its power over the human being, to lure him away from the cares of the world into a land of perpetual present. A garden is not wholly for pleasure, for it refreshes" (Jellicoe, 1995). Being in the presence of verdant greenery is a refreshing and relaxing experience. That said, we must also acknowledge the realities that come with taking care of your plants. Creating a successful indoor garden will require time and effort on your part so that all of your houseplants' needs are met. Just because indoor gardening will demand your labor and attention does not mean that tending to your houseplants needs to be frustrating or stressful. If a sound foundation for an amazing indoor garden relies on planning, then stress-free plant maintenance relies on developing a well-thought-out, well-organized, and consistent routine. Developing such a routine alleviates you from worrying about providing for your plants' needs since you already have your gardening tasks mapped out. Furthermore, a clear schedule will give you the time to observe your plants, monitor their health, and look out for any signs of pests or diseases. Finally, having a plant care schedule will help you improve as an indoor gardener. You can witness how your gardening practices like watering or fertilizing impact your houseplants, giving you a clear idea of what works and what doesn't. In this chapter, we will identify the key tasks and activities that will comprise your weekly, monthly, and seasonal routine. We will also discuss some ways that you can troubleshoot problems when they arise, thus being able to come up with both short-term and long-term solutions to resolve these issues. Finally, we will explore approaches and practices to indoor gardening that promote mental health and well-being, so that we can truly be "refreshed" by our indoor garden.

Maintenance Routines

Weekly Plant Care Activities

Two main plant maintenance tasks need to be accomplished weekly: (1) watering; and (2) pruning. The majority of indoor plants do not need to be watered daily. Watering your houseplants every day runs the serious risk of overwatering, impeding root respiration, and essentially "suffocating" your plants. Instead, it is better to conduct what is known as "deep watering" once or twice every week. Deep watering is the most efficient way to water your plants, which involves soaking the soil until it can hold no more water. This is very easy to do with indoor plants, as they are most likely to be growing in containers. Just add water to the soil until you hear excess water being expelled from the container's drainage hole, and you see that the topmost part of the soil is secreting excess water. This should meet your houseplants' water needs for the week. Since there are bound to be variations among individual plants, do observe the soil during your first week of deep watering to see if it dries out. If this happens, you may need to deep water the plants again to ensure that they have enough moisture to absorb from the soil.

Pruning is the other essential weekly task in maintaining your houseplants. Pruning selectively cuts off stems and branches of the plant to encourage further growth, remove dead or decaying sections of the plant, and maintain a particular aesthetic. Your annuals need to receive regular pruning since they will grow from seed to mature plants within the span of one or two seasons. The rapid growth of annuals makes them more receptive to pruning and its benefits, particularly in stimulating your desired growth patterns. For example, several varieties of New York asters require judicious pruning in the early summer so that they can bloom at the end of the season. We will be discussing specific pruning techniques in Chapter 5, but for now, your weekly pruning routine will most likely involve "pinching" stems and emerging flower buds in your flowering annuals to produce denser clusters of flowers in full bloom. Since perennials grow more slowly, they do not need as much pruning and can be done seasonally or even annually.

Other activities that you can incorporate into your weekly schedule are dusting the leaves of your houseplants and inspecting for pests and diseases. If you live in dust-prone areas such as urban centers or a sandy region, dust can accumulate on the leaves of your plants. This restricts the amount of light they can use and can block off their stomata. You can remove dust from the leaves by wiping them off with a piece of damp cloth. Just be careful with specimens that have fragile and delicate leaves, and make sure that the leaves are dry afterward. Inspecting your plants for pests or diseases every week allows you to catch these problems early on, making resolving these issues significantly easier.

Monthly Tasks for Optimal Health

The most important monthly task in plant maintenance is applying fertilizer and/or supplements to make sure that your houseplants are receiving the right kind and amount of nutrients. The majority of commercially available fertilizers—both organic and inorganic—are of the "slow release" type, which means that they release their nutrients for plants to absorb over a relatively long period. This is to prevent the phenomenon known as fertilizer burn, where the roots can dry out as excessive nutrients in the soil draw moisture away from the roots as part of the process of nutrient absorption. The risk of fertilizer burn is also the reason why you must be careful not to apply too much fertilizer to your houseplants. You can find the ideal amounts of fertilizer to use for specific plants online or by consulting with your local gardening store or plant nursery. There are some signs exhibited by your houseplants that should give you an idea if they are not getting enough of a particular macronutrient. Look for the following effects during your monthly fertilizing routine and make the appropriate adjustments in your plants' fertilizer and/or supplements.

- **Light green or yellowing mature foliage** – your plant may need more nitrogen since nitrogen is the principal macronutrient that promotes leaf growth.
- **Light green foliage with dark green veins** – your plant may need a higher percentage of potassium in its fertilizer.
- **Slow budding, flowering, and fruiting** – another indicator that your plant may need more potassium.
- **Older leaves turn purple and newer leaves have a dull, dark green color** – your plant may need more phosphorous.

A monthly, comprehensive check of the health of your plants is also good gardening practice. Dead leaves and branches should mainly appear near the base of the plant, as these are older sections that naturally wilt away as the plant continues to grow. Do a more thorough examination for pests and diseases, looking for potential insect colonies at the bottom of your houseplants' containers, underneath the soil, or within the immediate vicinity of your indoor garden. Make sure that your plants continue to receive the ideal amount of light; there may be changes in the light access in your home that are causing over- or under-exposure. Finally, inspect any of the automated systems you have installed to see if they are working properly. Discovering any problems in your watering or temperature and humidity control systems will save you the headache of finding out too late that they have failed and that you need to immediately resolve these issues if you want your plants to survive.

Seasonal Adjustments

The end of a season is both an exciting and demanding time for gardeners. This is the period where you can make significant changes to your indoor garden, trying out new things or making adjustments based on your successes and failures from the previous season. For your annuals, the end of summer and winter are especially important. At the end of summer, most of your flowering annuals are likely to have completed their life cycle, and now you have to decide if you want to replace them with fall and winter species. Similarly, at the end of winter, you will have to decide on which annuals you'll be having for the spring and summer seasons. These periods are a good time to take stock of how your annuals have done for this year. Take notes as to which species were successful and fit your vision for your indoor garden, and which ones you had difficulty growing or that ended up clashing with your desired aesthetic. Whether it is the end of summer or the end of winter, you will have to prepare the soil for the next batch of annuals you will grow. As such, this is a great time to amend the soil in your indoor garden, adding the right fertilizer mix to replace lost nutrients. There are many cheap home soil testing kits available that let you know the amounts of the three main macronutrients left in the soil—nitrogen, phosphorus, and potassium—so that you can amend the soil appropriately.

There are also several maintenance tasks you can do for your perennials at the end of a season. It is ideal to prune your perennials during this time, either by thinning them to manage their foliage or to promote growth in the next season. Late in autumn, some perennial species like peonies and daylilies will also need pruning, especially if they are located in an area of your home that has exposure to the winter cold. Most perennials also go dormant during the winter season, so at the end of fall, you might want to protect their bedding from the cold and frost. An easy and inexpensive way to accomplish this is to use mulch made up of woodchips, sawdust, or cardboard. Mulch will regulate the temperature of the soil and protect your dormant perennials from being damaged by frost. Of course, if your indoor garden is located in a climate-controlled space, you don't need to use mulch to protect your dormant houseplants, though it is still a good idea to cover their containers. Plants are sensitive to light and keeping them illuminated over the winter when they are supposed to be in darkness may impact their growth in spring.

Troubleshooting Common Issues

Recognizing and Treating Overwatering and Underwatering

Overwatering and under-watering are quite common mistakes even among experienced gardeners. Beginner gardeners think that they have to water their houseplants every day, impeding root respiration and washing away vital nutrients in the soil. Unforeseen changes in temperature or humidity might increase the rate of evaporation in your indoor garden, which leads to under-watering. Watering setups might malfunction, resulting in your plant containers receiving too much or too little moisture. As we discussed in Chapter 2, the soil serves as a good indicator that you are providing the right amount of water to your houseplants. If the topsoil is still moist—not wet or soaked—then you don't have to water your plants, especially if you utilize deep watering. You can check if the deeper layers of the soil are still moist by dipping your fingers two inches deep into the growth medium. That said, if the soil has become completely dry to the point of hardening, then it needs to be watered. If the soil has completely dried out, you can restore moisture absorption by submerging the entire container in a larger container filled with water for an hour. If the container is too large, you can use sticks or skewers to poke holes into the soil, then fill those holes with water.

Dealing With Yellowing Leaves and Brown Spots

Yellowing leaves and the appearance of brown spots are warning signs that your plant's health is deteriorating. Take these indicators seriously and conduct a thorough inspection of your houseplant. To treat the plant, you must identify the source of the problem. There are several possible causes of yellowing leaves and brown spots:

- Overwatering
- Under-watering
- Pest infestations
- Onset of diseases, especially fungal types
- Too much exposure to sunlight

It would be a good idea to prune the leaves that have gone yellow or have developed brown spots. These leaves are likely to die anyway, and keeping them on the plant will only impede growth. Moreover, if the plant has a disease, removing the infected parts may help prevent the disease from spreading throughout the plant.

Addressing Fungal Infections and Root Rot

Root rot is a result of a fungal infection attacking the roots of the plant, resulting in the rotting and eventual death of the root system. Fungal infections that cause root rot usually develop after overwatering. Fungal spores deep in the soil will typically remain dormant. However, when the soil is overwatered, the wet and warm conditions stimulate the fungal spores to start growing, which then attack the plant's roots to derive nutrients. To check for root rot, you must inspect the roots. Your monthly check-up is the perfect time to do this inspection. Using your hand trowel, carefully dig around the base of your plant and look at the extent of the root system. Remove the plant from the soil, then shake off any excess dirt to observe the roots. Healthy plants will have firm, white roots; the presence of root rot is indicated by the roots turning brown and having a soft, "mushy" texture. If your plant has indeed contracted root rot, you will have to remove the infected sections with your shears or a small pair of scissors. Then, you'll have to replant in a new container, ensuring there is proper drainage and that you do not overwater your houseplant.

The Zen of Houseplant Care

Mindful Gardening Practices

One of the benefits of indoor gardening involves the positive effects tending to plants has on human beings' mental health. A recent study by researchers from Wayne University and Michigan State University found that gardening improved mood and reduced stress, particularly among those living in urban spaces (Beavers, et al., 2022). Don't view taking care of your houseplants as additional work, but rather as leisure time where you can relax and take your mind off the stresses of daily life. Another mindful gardening practice that you can employ is to play meditative, calming music in your indoor garden. The study conducted by Dr. Mousumi Das discovered that music actually has a positive effect on the growth and overall health of plants. In particular, heavily rhythmic music that characterizes Buddhist pirith chanting and chanting mantras in Vedic rituals enhanced stem, leaf, and root length in plants (Das, 2023). As such, playing these types of music in your indoor garden will not only let you enjoy their calming, meditative effects, but they will also promote good health among your houseplants.

Cultivating Patience

The poet May Sarton once wrote, "Everything that slows us down and forces patience, everything that sets us back into the slow circles of nature, is a help. Gardening is an instrument of grace" (Streep & Glover, 2003). Anyone who has had to take care of plants knows very well that it does indeed "force patience"—it can be very frustrating to find that those azaleas you've been trying to grow all spring and summer end up failing to bloom, and the miniature lemon tree you've been doting over refuses to bear harvestable fruit. As we've discussed in the various plant maintenance routines you can develop, the actual, direct actions you can take to care for your plants aren't really very labor intensive. As such, the majority of the time you will just be waiting for your plants to grow.

This wait can test your patience, and you may start to wonder if there are things you can do to make your green companions reach their full potential more quickly. My advice is to acknowledge that gardening requires us as human beings to adapt to nature's time, rather than forcing nature to adapt to ours. No amount of additional fertilizer or amendments will make your houseplants grow faster, and obsessing over providing for your plants' needs will ultimately be unproductive. Instead, relish the moments of peace and calm with your plants, and appreciate how they grow day by day. Observe the miraculous changes they undergo from week to week. Keep a gardening journal where you draw or describe your plants at each stage of their growth. When you experience failures in your annuals or one of your perennials does not make it, instead of being frustrated, reflect on the things that went wrong and how you can do better next time. In abiding by nature's time and learning patience, we extend our love and care to our plants, and we also grow as individuals.

Enjoying the Journey

At the heart of creating a mindful, stress-free plant care routine is finding the joy in gardening. The greenery inside your home confers many benefits, from beautifying your surroundings to producing fruits and vegetables for you and your loved ones to evoke a calm, relaxing atmosphere where you can escape from the troubles of the world. Reflect on your gardening experiences and determine which aspects of tending to your houseplants make you happy. By identifying the elements of indoor gardening that give you joy, you can make plans in the future that highlight these wonderful elements. Does having colorful plants in your living room bring you happiness? Then next spring, try growing more species of long-blooming plants like petunias and marigolds. Do you enjoy the challenge of growing exotic, tropical plants? Successfully adding a flourishing Bird of Paradise plant to your collection will give you this sense of accomplishment and satisfaction. Are you the most interested and engaged in gardening when designing the arrangements for your plant boxes? Then allocate a day or two at the end of the spring and summer seasons to just perfectly design and organize your plants. By reflecting on what brings you pleasure, satisfaction, and fulfillment in tending to your houseplants, you will continuously find joy in gardening every single day.

4

PEST CONTROL AND MANAGEMENT

P ests are a problem that all gardeners must contend with at some point in their green journey. In many cases, pests are a nuisance that makes tending to your plants more inconvenient. However, when left unchecked, a pest infestation may become a serious issue, threatening your houseplants' very survival. Dealing with pests is generally more manageable when you are caring for an indoor garden, as your house or apartment functions like a fortress that keeps out insects, birds, and other creatures that want to feed on your plants. Still, making sure that your indoor garden remains pest-free can feel like an ongoing battle, with you trying to prevent any of your greenery's enemies from invading and conquering your home. To win against these hostile organisms, we must first know which pests are most likely to threaten indoor plants. We must understand which parts of the plants they target, which gardening practices invite their arrival, and how they come to harm our plants. With this information, we can employ preventative measures to keep pests from getting to our plants in the first place. If pests do manage to invade our indoor gardens, there are several do-it-yourself methods to either minimize their damage or eliminate them. I would suggest that you resort to chemical pesticides as a last resort. Pests may be dangerous to your plants, but remember that these are still living creatures and are a part of nature's order. We will discuss the safe, effective, and ecologically-minded ways to use pesticides at the conclusion of this chapter.

Identifying Common Pests

Aphids, Mealybugs, and Scale Insects

The most common pests you will have to contend with as an indoor gardener are aphids, mealybugs, and insects known as "scales." All three houseplant pests are characterized by their small size, which makes them difficult to spot when they attach to your clothes or have infected new houseplants that you are bringing into your home. Aphids, mealybugs, and scales all feed on sap, causing damage when they pierce the leaves and stems to drain away vital nutrients from the plant. These three common houseplant pests are also notorious for reproducing very quickly. Preventative measures are the best means of controlling them because once a few of them infect your plants, it is only a short time before their populations grow to a size that becomes unmanageable.

Aphids

Aphids are insects with pear- or tear-shaped bodies and long legs, about two to four millimeters in length. Most aphids are colored green or brown, though some also appear yellow, orange, or black, depending on the plant that they feed on. Aphids harm your plants in two ways: first, they use their long, piercing mouths to suck on the plant's vital sap; second, they release a fluid known as honeydew, which provides nutrients for many kinds of fungus to grow on the plant. Most aphid species not only reproduce very quickly but also do so without requiring mating. In indoor conditions, adult female aphids can give birth to their young at a rate of three to six aphids a week. As such, even a few aphids that make their way into your indoor garden can quickly become a difficult pest infestation to manage.

Mealybugs

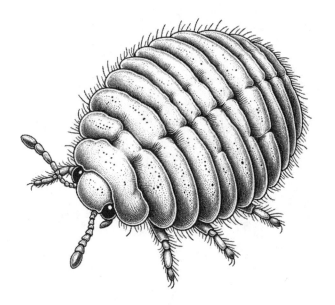

Mealybugs are oval-shaped insects with multiple, short, waxy filaments surrounding the edge of their body. Their average size ranges from 3 to 4.5 millimeters, and appear dull pink or yellow. Like aphids, mealybugs inflict damage on plants by piercing leaves and stems to suck on the sap, as well as secreting honeydew that promotes the growth of harmful fungi. Many species of mealybugs also secrete wax as a protective covering. The females of a very common species of mealybug in North America, the Citrus mealybug (Planococcus citri), can lay 300 to 600 eggs once they reach maturity in a period of six weeks to two months. The females immediately die after laying their eggs, but in ideal indoor conditions, this means a massive explosion of the mealybug population in your indoor garden. The adult mealybugs are not the pests; rather, the nymphs of this insect during the feeding stage are the ones that can cause significant damage to plants because of their sheer number.

Scales

Scales are roughly circular insects that are either brown, red, or white. Different scale species vary in size quite widely, with some as small as one to two millimeters, while others can grow to five millimeters in diameter. These pests get their name from the hard, waxy covering they develop when they mature. Unlike aphids or mealybugs, scales are sedentary pests—once they begin feeding on the plant's sap, they root themselves in a single place. They then secrete wax to protect themselves, as well as honeydew that can cover large portions of the plant's leaves and stems. Depending on the species, adult female scales can lay up to 2000 eggs, which hatch into young insects in one to three weeks. Scales are notoriously difficult to deal with once they have infested a plant, as their waxy covering does protect them from the common ways to deal with plant pests.

Spider Mites and Fungus Gnats

Spider mites and fungus gnats are not as common as piercing-sucking pests, only appearing when particular environmental conditions occur. They also damage your plants differently from aphids, mealybugs, and scales. You shouldn't underestimate spider mites and fungus gnats, however, as they can still prove fatal to your houseplants when left untreated.

Spider Mites

Spider mites are very tiny, oval-shaped arachnids that primarily feed on the underside of plants' leaves. In the United States, the most common type of spider mite to infest indoor gardens is the two-spotted spider mite, which is green to translucent in color. The two-spotted spider mite is less than a millimeter in diameter, which, coupled with their green color, makes them difficult to find in your plants. While spider mites also feed on plant sap causing tiny yellow spots on the leaves, they also harm your plants with the webs they produce in their colonies. Spider mites thrive in hot and dry environments, as these conditions kill many of their natural predators while also accelerating the growth of their young. They can grow from eggs to adults in as little as five days in these conditions. Since adult females can lay 300 eggs at a time, a large spider mite colony can quickly overwhelm your indoor garden.

Fungus gnats

Adult fungus gnats are black, flying insects that resemble mosquitos. These mature fungus gnats are not the pests, however, as they are harmless to both plants and humans. The adults only live for a week, and their sole purpose is to reproduce. The females will typically lay around 300 eggs over the course of a week, and then die. It is the fungus gnat larvae that do considerable damage to your houseplants, eating the roots and contributing to the onset of root rot. The larvae are larger than the adults, about seven millimeters in length, and have a distinctive black head and segmented body. Wet, overwatered soil is the ideal environment for fungus gnat larvae. The larvae will feed on the roots over a two-week period, then transform into a pupa that in three days will become winged fungus gnat adults.

Bacterial and Fungal Diseases

Many plant diseases are caused by malnutrition and extreme environmental conditions. But there are also many diseases caused by the infections of bacterial and fungal pathogens. Unlike regular pests, you can't employ many preventative measures to protect your houseplants from contracting these diseases. There are bacteria everywhere, with most types of bacteria contributing to the healthy growth of your greenery. Similarly, fungal spores are microscopic and prevalent in all climates and regions, so you can't prevent fungus from potentially growing in your indoor garden. The best thing you can do is recognize the symptoms of a bacterial or fungal disease to use the correct treatment to cure your houseplants. Here are three common bacterial and fungal diseases that affect plants grown indoors.

Bacterial and Fungal Leaf Spots

Both bacteria and fungus can cause leaf spots that hamper your houseplants' ability to create food. The main difference between these two types of infections is that bacteria result in black, wet spots on the leaves, while fungus produces dry, brown, or reddish spots. Fungal leaf spots are easier to manage, as they tend to be localized. Typically, removing the infected leaves should prevent further spread of the disease. Bacterial leaf spots can also be localized, and so removing the leaves with the spots is an effective treatment. Sometimes, however, the infection is systemic, affecting the entire plant. In this situation, it is unfortunately too late to save the plant. What you can do is discard the sick houseplant to prevent the disease from spreading throughout your garden.

Powdery Mildew

The species of fungus called Oidium is responsible for the powdery mildew disease. The disease gets its name from the white, powdery growths that appear throughout the plant. While powdery mildew is quite prolific in North America, it is not as dangerous as other plant diseases. Oidium thrives in cool, moist environments, and changing the conditions in your indoor garden should stop the disease from progressing. If only a few white growths have started to appear, you can also remove these sections of the plant as a treatment.

Root Rot

Several fungal species cause root rot: Rhizoctonia, Pythium, Botrytis, Phytophthora, Alternaria, and Sclerotinia. These fungi "feed" on the starchy roots of the plant, which results in soft, mushy root sections as the root system is drained of its nutrients. It can be difficult to recognize the onset of root rot, as the fungi grow underneath the soil and will only be visible if you dig up and examine the roots. If you do manage to discover that some of the roots have succumbed to root rot, you can still remove them and prevent the spread of the disease. At some point, though, the root rot may already be so pervasive throughout the root system that it will be too late to save the plant. Overwatering significantly increases the risk of root rot, as it provides hydration to the fungi and cools down the temperature of the soil to the ideal conditions for fungal growth.

Natural Remedies and Prevention

Preventing Infestations

The old saying "an ounce of prevention is worth more than a pound of cure" is true in the case of managing pests and diseases in your indoor garden. The majority of preventative practices that you can employ are very easy to do and will save you from what could be an enormous amount of time, money, and stress it would cost to treat your plants. Furthermore, most of these practices are already part of your plant maintenance routine. Here are seven preventative measures you can take to protect your houseplants from being susceptible to pest infestations and disease:

- Make sure to maintain the ideal environmental conditions for your plants. Always check that the temperature, humidity, and lighting in your indoor garden remain consistent, as sudden changes will be detrimental to your plants and result in conditions that encourage pests and diseases.

- Inspect your plants for signs and symptoms of pests and diseases. A lot of pests and diseases are easily dealt with if you catch them early on. As we established in Chapter 3, a monthly comprehensive examination of your plants is good gardening practice.
- Water your plants properly. As we've discussed earlier, many pests and diseases love moist environments. Having the soil in your plant containers retain too much moisture invites infestations. Also, avoid splashing water onto the leaves and stems of your plants when watering, as these can be vectors for fungal and bacterial growth.
- Change your clothes before tending to your garden, especially if you've recently been outdoors. The eggs and larvae of many pests, as well as fungal spores, can cling to your clothes when you go outside. A quick change of clothes will reduce the risk of infestation or infections from external sources.
- Take advantage of growing plants indoors by minimizing your garden's outside exposure. You've already set up your indoor garden to have ideal growing conditions, so there is no need to expose your houseplants to the risk of pests from the outside world.
- Use fresh garden soil when refilling your plant containers. Used garden soil could harbor the eggs of harmful insects and fungal spores. If you are repotting new seedlings, check the soil that comes with the young plant for potential pests.
- Grow new plants separately from the rest of your indoor garden for one to two weeks. During this isolation period, you can check if any unwanted organisms are dormant in

the plant, preventing pests and diseases from spreading to your other houseplants.

DIY Pest Control Solutions

If pests do manage to infest your houseplants, do not despair—there are still several things you can do to protect your plants from injury and get rid of the hostile invaders in your indoor garden. These do-it-yourself options do not require the application of chemical pesticides nor the services of a professional to utilize. You can try these DIY solutions out, and if they don't work, then you can consult with a horticulturist or botanist to combat the infestation. Let us begin with pest control practices that target specific types of pests:

- Aphids, mealybugs, and scales can be physically removed from the plant, either by pruning the infested areas or by spraying them off with water. Just make sure to wipe the leaves and stems dry afterward, to prevent fungus or bacteria from growing in the moist areas of your plant.
- Since fungus gnat larvae feed on the starchy roots of your plants, placing a slice of raw potato on the soil will attract them to the surface to feed.
- Spider mites and aphids can be killed by using a soap and water mixture applied to the infested areas.

There are also natural pest control products that you can buy to help you eliminate the pests that have managed to invade your indoor garden. Do remember to follow the instructions on the packaging to apply these products correctly:

- Neem oil is an all-natural insecticide that is used as the key ingredient in many commercial pesticides. It reduces insect feeding and acts as an insect repellant. Do note that because neem oil targets insects in general, it may also harm any beneficial insects living in your indoor garden.
- Horticultural oils are natural pesticides that work by suffocating the pests damaging your plants. Excess horticultural oil quickly evaporates and is generally safe for humans and pets. Be careful in applying horticultural oil, though, since it can cause skin irritation in some individuals.

Using Beneficial Insects

There are many creatures that gardeners consider to be beneficial to the health and safety of their plants. Unfortunately, many of these beneficial animals are more prevalent in outdoor gardens. Centipedes, bees, and even toads and birds are all-natural predators of common plant pests, but these animals cannot really realistically have access to your indoor garden. The good news is that there are several insects that you can introduce to your houseplants that will help keep pests under control.

- **Ladybugs:** Ladybugs are great insects for protecting your flowering annuals from soft-bodied pests like aphids and mealybugs. If you are growing your flowering houseplants near windows or a balcony, ladybugs will naturally be attracted to them, particularly during summer and fall. Let them stay in your indoor garden to feed on potential pests.

- **Cryptolaemus montrouzieri, "Mealybug Destroyer":**
As its name suggests, the mealybug destroyer feeds on
mealybugs, making it an excellent, non-pesticidal option
for dealing with a mealybug infestation. Live adult
mealybug destroyers can be bought relatively cheaply in
organic gardening stores and online retailers.

- **Steinernema feltiae and Steinernema carpocapsae Nematodes:** Nematodes are microscopic roundworms, and several species feed on the larvae of common indoor plant pests like fungus gnat larvae. Many gardening stores offer these beneficial nematodes for sale. Nematode packets are typically bought frozen, then applied on the soil of your houseplants, and "activated" with water. While nematodes have a short lifespan, they can remain in "stasis" for long periods while frozen, so you can keep them in your freezer for use when soil pests appear in your indoor garden.

Chemical Options and When to Use Them

The agricultural sector of the United States applies an estimated 900 million pounds of chemical pesticides every year (Bauder, Wardle, & Waskom, 2020). In many ways, chemical pesticides are an important part of the nation's agricultural production, a testament to their efficacy in controlling plant pests. However, chemical pesticides have many known detrimental effects on plant and human health, as well as damaging impacts on ecosystems. As an indoor gardener, it can be tempting to use chemical pesticides immediately to get rid of pests that are damaging your precious houseplants. This is not ideal, as chemical pesticides have many detrimental effects on your indoor garden and houseplants:

- Chemical pesticides can degrade the soil quality in your garden: upsetting the balance of nutrients available in the soil, killing the microorganisms that play key roles in root absorption, and drying out the growth medium.
- Pesticides are likely to kill beneficial insects that prey on particular pests. You may eliminate a current infestation, only to have it replaced with a new type of pest because the beneficial insects are no longer present to keep the new invaders under control.
- Chemical pesticides are harmful to humans and pets. You will have to take extra precautions to ensure that your family and your pets do not get poisoned or injured by the pesticide.
- Unless disposed of properly, pesticides will end up harming marine wildlife and local ecosystems. Manufacturing chemical pesticides also has a large carbon footprint, so purchasing them contributes to damage to the environment.

There will be situations when the benefits of efficacy and rapid action will outweigh the potential negative impacts of chemical pesticides. In such cases, it is very important that you know the different types of pesticides available, their use cases, how to safely and effectively apply them, and how to minimize their ecological harm.

Understanding Chemical Treatments

Chemical pesticides can either be in liquid or powdered forms, depending on the application vector. Liquid pesticides are used when you want to retain moisture in the soil or the plant itself, as many of the active ingredients in pesticides will draw out moisture and result in faster water evaporation. Solid or powdered pesticides are used when the target pest thrives in wet environments and the plant is hardy enough to survive in drier conditions. Almost all chemical pesticides that are applied in liquid form are concentrates, meaning you will have to dilute them with water. You must follow the instructions carefully in the packaging. Pay particular attention to the precise volumes or weights described in the instructions, and use weighing scales and measuring cups to achieve accurate measurements. Pesticides can also be grouped depending on the type of organism they are meant to control:

- **Insecticide** – targets insects
- **Miticide** – targets mites/arachnids
- **Herbicide** – targets weeds and unwanted plants
- **Fungicide** – targets fungi/mold

Chemical pesticides also have differing modes of action, which refers to how a pesticide manages and controls the pest population. As we covered earlier, neem oil works by suppressing the feeding capabilities of piercing-sucking insects like aphids and mealybugs. Other pesticides suffocate pests as their mode of action. The packaging of the pesticide will indicate which mode of action it specifically uses. This is important information because you do not want to apply pesticides with the same modes of action at the same time or consecutively.

Safe and Effective Use of Pesticides

- Follow the instructions for preparing and applying chemical pesticides very carefully. These instructions will also include safety precautions that will prevent injury and contamination—pay close attention to these precautions and inform anyone else living in your home about them.
- Treat small areas of your plant as much as possible, focusing on the most heavily infested areas. If you have many plants in your indoor garden, limit the application of pesticides to the ones you know have been infested. Ideally, you will want to isolate these infested plants for treatment with pesticides.
- If you are using multiple pesticides in your garden, make sure to rotate the application of pesticides that have different modes of action. Applying pesticides with the same mode of action consecutively can result in the pests developing a resistance to the pesticide.
- Always use liquid pesticides immediately after preparing. Using liquid pesticides after being left overnight results in reduced and inconsistent efficacy.
- The ideal time for applying pesticides is in the early morning and early evening when temperatures are cooler. This allows the pesticides to evaporate before they become

too hot, preventing your plants from losing too much moisture.

Being Environmentally Responsible

The best way to be environmentally responsible when using chemical pesticides is to minimize their application. Make sure you only purchase the amount of pesticide necessary to treat your houseplants to avoid having to throw out excess pesticides you weren't able to use. The U.S. Environmental Protection Agency (EPA) classifies all unused chemical pesticides as hazardous waste, and they should be treated as such during disposal. Never pour unused liquid pesticides or rinse water down the drain, as they will eventually end up contaminating local ecosystems. In the U.S. you can call the hotline 1-800-CLEANUP (1-800-253-2687) to contact your local household hazardous waste disposal site—they can tell you where to bring your unused pesticides or used pesticide containers for proper disposal. Note that these disposal practices are mandated by federal law, and some states have stricter legislation when it comes to pesticide use and disposal. Improper disposal of chemical pesticides is not only environmentally irresponsible, it may even be illegal in some cases.

MAKE A DIFFERENCE WITH YOUR REVIEW

PLANT SEEDS OF KINDNESS WITH YOUR REVIEW

"The true gardener, like a good artist, is not the one who puts the most into their work, but the one who gets the most out of it."

UNKNOWN

Did you know that people who give without expecting anything in return tend to be happier and more fulfilled? That's what we're aiming for in our journey together. And I have a special request for you...

Would you help someone you've never met, just for the joy of it?

Who is this mysterious person, you ask? They're a lot like you used to be. Eager to learn about houseplants, wanting to make their home greener, and looking for guidance, but still trying to figure out where to start.

Many people choose books based on their covers and what others say about them. So here's my request on behalf of a budding house-plant enthusiast you've never met:

Please help them by leaving a review of this book. Your review could help...

- ...one more person create a calming green space in their home.
- ...one more family enjoy the beauty of nature indoors.
- ...one more student learn about the wonders of plant care.

- ...one more green thumb discover their passion.
- ...one more dream of a lush indoor garden come true.

To spread this joy and make a difference, all you have to do is...take a moment to...

leave a review.

Just scan the QR code below to share your thoughts:

Thank you from the bottom of my heart. Now, let's get back to our green journey.

Your biggest fan, Natalia Kozlova

PS - Here's a fun fact: Sharing something valuable with someone enhances your value in their eyes. If this book will help another plant enthusiast, why not share it with them? Let's spread the love for houseplants together!

5

ADVANCED CARE TECHNIQUES

R osemary Verey is one of Britain's most celebrated garden designers. In 1996, she received the Victoria Medal of Honour from the Royal Horticultural Society, which is the highest accolade one can receive from the institution. Verey is most known for her work on her home garden at Barnsley House in Gloucestershire. Her home garden was opened to the public in the 1970s, after which it welcomed 30,000 visitors every year. Having worked for over fifty years cultivating her Barnsley House garden, Verey describes her approach to gardening: "Although I arrived here more than fifty years ago, I constantly try to see the garden with new eyes. This is the wonderful thing about gardening: trees are ever-growing taller, shrubs are developing, and ground cover is taking over. The scene changes and every year has its own character" (Verey, Lord, & Wills, 1995). Verey's success is rooted in her ability to grow as a gardener alongside the growth of her garden. To elevate your indoor gardening prowess, you will also need to grow —grow in knowledge, skills, and experience in tending to your plants. In this chapter we will explore different techniques and practices that will facilitate this growth, allowing you to provide expert-level care to your houseplants and bring your indoor garden to the next level.

Propagation and Pruning

Propagating Houseplants from Cuttings

Many gardeners choose to learn plant propagation as their entry point into the next phase of their gardening journey. In gardening, propagation refers to the growing of a new generation of plants from an older generation. Propagation can either be sexual or asexual. The most common type of sexual propagation is growing a new plant from seeds produced by your older plants. The most common type of asexual propagation—and the one many gardeners learn as a key, advanced practice in the hobby—is growing a new plant from a cutting, or a part of the old plant. Woody and herbaceous plants, perennials, and annuals can all be grown from cuttings. Stem tip cuttings and medial cuttings are the easiest to do.

To propagate a plant from a tip cutting, follow this procedure:

1. Choose a new, young stem of the plant you want to propagate and cut it two to six inches from the terminal/end bud and above a stem node.
2. Remove the leaves near the bottom of the stem cutting, especially those that will come in contact with or be buried under the soil.
3. Insert the stem cutting into fresh garden soil at a deep enough level that it can support itself. There must be at least one stem node above the surface of the soil. This stem node will be the growth site for new stems and leaves.

To propagate a plant from a medial cutting, follow this procedure:

1. Make a first cut above a stem node on one of your plant's stems that you want to propagate.
2. Make a second cut two to six inches below the first cut, also above a node.
3. Remove the leaves near the second cut, as this will be the "end" of the cutting you will be inserting into the soil.
4. Insert the stem cutting into fresh garden soil deep enough so that the cutting can support itself, making sure the stem node is well above the surface of the soil.

Do note that some species like African violets, coleus, and pothos do better when the cuttings are first grown in water rather than being directly inserted into the soil. For these plants, place the cutting in a container filled with water, preferably one that is transparent so that you can see when roots start to appear. Replace the water in the container every week or so and within a month the cutting should have developed a robust enough root system to be replanted into soil.

Pruning for Growth

We mentioned in Chapter 3 how a good plant maintenance routine involves regular pruning. The primary goal during your weekly or monthly pruning (depending on the type of plant) routine is to remove dead leaves, flowers, and stems from the plant. Not only does this result in a more beautiful, cleaner look for your houseplants, but this also promotes healthy growth. Dead sections that remain attached to the plant can still draw water and nutrients, and so removing them tells your plant to divert these resources towards still-growing sections. Pruning dead and wilted parts also improves air circulation around the plant and helps prevent the growth of fungi and bacteria that could lead to diseases. Beyond just cleaning up dead sections of your houseplants, the primary pruning technique you will be using on your indoor plants to stimulate growth will be heading or heading back.

Heading or heading back refers to the removal of a currently growing shoot to a bud or node. This is a versatile technique that allows you to direct how your houseplants will grow and define their shape and form to your liking. Heading can be employed in the following use cases:

- Encouraging your flowering annuals to produce denser clusters of flowers - Heading the "leaders" or the youngest stems of your annuals before their blooming season will encourage vigorous growth just below where you made your cut, causing more flowers to bloom in these areas.
- Thicken "leggy" stems – Annuals and perennials can grow long, delicate stems that have few buds or nodes that would allow for further growth. By pruning these "leggy" stems, the plant is stimulated to grow a thicker, more robust stem and produce nodes that would lead to more branches and flowers.
- Improve the foliage of shrubs – Ornamental shrubs look best when their foliage is lush and dense. However, this can prevent light and proper air circulation from reaching the inner parts of the shrub, preventing growth. By pruning the outermost stems and leaves of the shrub, its foliage is given the chance to develop a fuller shape.
- Spring-flowering perennials are stimulated to produce more flowers – When spring-flowering perennials like foxgloves are pruned after their first bloom, the next bloom will be more vigorous.

There are several things to remember when heading your plants. First, make sure to use sharp pruning scissors and shears, as you want to make clean cuts on your plant. Dull pruning tools will crush the areas where you make your cuts, which in turn creates an environment for bacteria and fungi to grow. Second, you should cut at a 45-degree angle just above a stem node or bud, as this allows any moisture to slide off the now-exposed area. The cut area will dry up and "heal" more quickly, and prevent any infections from occurring due to moisture buildup. Third, clean your pruning tools regularly, especially if you are moving on to prune a different plant. Plant sap residue is bound to remain on the edges and surface of your pruning shears, which may become a vector for diseases.

Creating Unique Arrangements

Many indoor gardeners grow their houseplants with the main goal of beautifying their homes. As such, the major appeal of the hobby is coming up with new ways to showcase their greenery, organizing and arranging them in various ways to complement the architecture of their residence, or creating a unified theme. A very popular approach to flower and ornamental plant arrangement follows what is known as the "thriller, filler, spiller" rule. This rule applies to plants grown in containers, which is what comprise most indoor gardens.

- In a single plant container, you would grow one "thriller" species—these are your tall and colorful flowering annuals —that would serve as the main attraction in the container. Examples of great thriller plants are dracaenas, irises, and snapdragons.
- "Fillers" refer to shorter plants that fill up the container to cover the soil. Good options for filler plants are alyssums, moss roses, and petunias.
- Spillers are typically vines that grow beyond the edges of your plant container, creating a sense of verdant lushness to the arrangement. Sweet potato vine and weeping jenny are great choices for spillers.

While using the thriller, filler, and spiller rule provides an easy way to create a beautiful and harmonious arrangement for your house-plants, you may want something different and unique. Here are several surprising plant arrangement ideas you can try if you are feeling more adventurous.

- **A Succulent Showcase:** Succulents are severely underrated among gardeners, as their fleshy, waxy leaves are easy to mistake as plastic and "fake." However, succulents come in a variety of interesting forms that allow you to play with visual textures in your indoor garden. A good combination to grow together in a plant container are flapjacks (Kalanchoe thyrsiflora), "spaghetti strap" agave, and "hope" peperomia. You can also make a cacti arrangement, perfect for homes with a more rustic aesthetic.

- **All Thrillers, No Fillers:** If you love your flashy flowering annuals, then this arrangement is for you. You can have a large container filled only with your most vibrant flowers of the season in full bloom. If the species you've chosen all bloom at roughly the same time, they can share the same soil in the container. However, you may want to grow the individual plants in separate, smaller containers when they are younger early in the season, then combine them in a larger container when they fully blossom. An all-thriller arrangement is perfect as the centerpiece of your living room, providing your guests with a colorful welcome into your home.

- **Growing a Living Wall:** A blank wall in your home is the perfect space to decorate with a living wall. A living wall arrangement has your greenery growing "vertically," as if they are framed like a painting. There are wall planting systems you can purchase, though you can make one yourself by taking a shallow plant container, growing vines and creepers in it, then hanging your setup on a wall. Deep watering your living wall should be more than enough to meet its needs, and you can have the unique feature of a natural work of art being exhibited in your home.

Air Layering and Bonsai

The Art of Air Layering

Air layering is a form of asexual propagation like growing a new plant from a cutting taken from an older plant. In air layering, a plant stem is induced into growing roots while it is still attached to the parent plant. Air layering is used to propagate plant species that do not grow well from cuttings, and do not produce shallow shoots that would enable simple layering—simple layering is when a shoot near the bottom of the parent plant is inserted into soil to grow roots and become a new plant. Plants that can be air-layered are acers, daphnes, hazels, magnolias, and variants of Ficus and Philodendron.

To propagate using air layering you will need the following:

- Sphagnum moss
- Rooting hormone compound
- Plastic wrap
- Gardener's twist tIes
- Knife

The procedures for air layering are relatively simple. It is best to conduct air layering during autumn or spring, as the cooler temperatures during these seasons are conducive to growth.

1. Examine the parent plant and choose a young stem—about one to two years old—that is healthy and straight. Remove the leaves and any side shoots from a six-inch to one-foot section of this stem.

2. Make a one-inch, angled cut through a leaf bud/node, creating a gap that goes through most of the stem.

3. Apply rooting hormone compound on the surface of the cut.

4. Moisten a small portion of your sphagnum moss and fill the space created by the cut with the moist moss.

5. Wrap the stem section you've cut loosely with your plastic wrap, then seal one end firmly with your twist tie. This should create a plastic sleeve covering the stem section.

6. Fill the plastic sleeve with more sphagnum moss to about 3 to 4 inches thick.

7. Seal the other end of the plastic sleeve with a gardener's twist tie.

8. Leave the plastic wrapping securely in place for up to a year. Check occasionally to look for roots growing through the sphagnum moss.

9. Once strong, thick roots are visible through the sphagnum moss, you can remove the plastic wrapping. Cut the stem section just below the rooting end.

10. Plant the stem section into the appropriate garden soil. Do not remove any moss that remains among the roots.

Exploring the World of Bonsai

Bonsai is the art of growing mature trees in containers. Bonsai is a Japanese word that translates to "to train in a tray," as the craft was developed in Japan based on the Chinese tradition of penjing, which is the art of creating natural landscape dioramas (Morris, 2011). The trees that were grown in containers used to be taken from nature, but as the availability of miniature trees became rare, Japanese gardeners began training young trees to maintain sizes suitable for growing in a container, as well as assuming precise, beautiful forms. The art of bonsai is considered an outdoor endeavor, but several tree species thrive indoors. Ficus, Carmona or Fukien tea, and the jade tree are popular indoor bonsai trees. These are your best options if you want to include bonsai in your indoor garden. Besides choosing the right species for your bonsai, you will want to decide on which bonsai style appeals to you and fits the aesthetics of your home. There are five basic styles of bonsai, with other styles being derivations or modifications of these basic styles (Muth, 2011).

- **Formal upright, or chokan:** The tree grows straight and vertical
- **Informal upright, or moyogi:** The tree grows vertically but has movement to its trunk line
- **Slanting, or shakan:** The tree leans to one side, but the topmost part remains within the area of the container
- **Semi-cascade, or han-kengai:** The tree leans over to the edge of its container
- **Full cascade, or kengai:** The tree leans over the edge of the container and then cascades downwards, dipping below the bottom edge of the container

To take care of your indoor bonsai, you must remember that they are still trees that need more resources than your annuals or perennial ornamental plants. Bonsai trees need to be exposed to direct sunlight for a few hours each day. They also need plenty of water—make sure to water them once the surface of the soil begins to dry out. Bonsai trees also need pruning more frequently than your other houseplants, removing branches that do not conform to the form prescribed by their particular style.

Growing your bonsai is a challenging undertaking, as this requires you to acquire and develop many skills in training the young tree to remain miniaturized and of a specific shape. Indeed, mastering the art of creating bonsai trees is a hobby in itself. There are many online resources available for you to explore this endeavor further, and you may want to check with your local plant nursery or gardening supply store to see if there are any bonsai clubs near your area. They should be able to offer you bonsai courses to provide you with the knowledge and skills you need.

Advanced Pruning Techniques

As we discussed earlier in this chapter, the most common and basic pruning technique you will be using in your indoor garden is heading or heading back. That said, heading can fulfill several functions beyond just stimulating the growth of dense clusters in your houseplants. Heading back can be used for tip-pruning, pinching, and shearing.

- **Tip-pruning:** The majority of heading cuts are meant for tip-pruning, which are cuts made on younger stems to promote dense growth. Deadheading, which is the removal of dead flowers and leaves, is also considered tip-pruning.
- **Pinching:** Pinching is a very simple procedure, which just involves nipping out a growing bud with your fingers. This is a form of heading back meant to dissuade a growing bud or very young stem from lengthening. This is perfect for avoiding "leggy" stems in your houseplants.
- **Shearing:** This use of heading back is intended to maintain the shape of a plant's foliage. For indoor gardeners, shearing is mainly done on ornamental shrubs and miniature trees. During shearing, individual stems or branches are not selected to be cut, but rather all parts of the plant that exceed the desired form of the foliage are removed.

Most of the other pruning techniques besides heading back are mostly used in outdoor gardens, as they are used to manage the yearly growth of trees and large woody perennials. If you are growing woody perennials or miniature fruit trees indoors, there are some pruning techniques that you will find useful.

- **Nicking and notching:** Nicking and notching are pruning techniques primarily used to train fruit trees and shrubs. Notching refers to making a wedge-shaped cut above a bud. This diverts sap flow to produce a stronger shoot from the bud. Nicking refers to making a wedge-shaped cut below the bud. This has the intended effect of making the bud weaker, for when you don't want a large branch to grow from a stem section.
- **Reduction cuts:** Reduction cuts are a type of pruning cut that does not leave a stub, which means that no vigorous growth will occur in the stem section. Reduction cuts are employed when you want to train a young shrub or tree— dissuading growth from strategic branches will ensure that the plant will grow in a particular direction.
- **Pollarding:** This is done exclusively to indoor trees, where the tree is cut back every few years to a basic framework of branches. Pollarding is essential in keeping an indoor tree to a manageable size. Do note that when pollarding you must never cut the trunk of the tree, only the branches. Branches and trunks are made up of different plant tissues. The tissue in the trunk cannot regenerate, so any cuts there will result in a "wound" that won't heal.

Mastering Indoor Plant Reproduction

Seed Starting and Germination

Whether you've bought a seed packet or taken seeds from your fruiting plants, you will need to germinate the seeds to start growing the plant. Inside the seed is the young plant in a dormant state. It is waiting for ideal conditions before it will become activated and start to grow. This "activation" of the young plant is germination. It is our job as gardeners to signal to the plant inside the seed that it is time to start growing. Four elements instigate germination: water, light, oxygen, and temperature.

- Water: All seeds require the presence of water to start germinating. As such, many seeds will require being soaked or even submerged in water to encourage germination.
- Light: Different seeds have varying light requirements for germination. Many seeds start germinating in the dark, as the absence of light indicates that the seed has been buried in the soil. At the same time, there are plants like begonia, browallia, impatiens, and lettuce whose seeds require light exposure to start germinating.
- Oxygen: The dormant plant inside the seed is not yet able to produce its food via photosynthesis, and so has to rely on the food supply it was provided with inside the seed, the cotyledons. To "burn" its food and have the energy to start growing, the dormant plant needs oxygen, not carbon dioxide. It is therefore a good idea to maintain good air circulation when germinating your seeds.
- Temperature: Like light requirements, the ideal temperature for germination varies depending on the plant species. That said, the majority of plants in temperate regions have ideal germination temperatures that fall within the range of 65 °F to 75 °F (Sideman, 2017).

Crossbreeding and Hybridization

In asexual propagation like growing new plants from stem cuttings, the new plant is effectively a "clone" of the parent plant—they have the same genes and therefore have the same characteristics While sexual plant propagation is more involved than asexual propagation, it does have the advantage of allowing you to crossbreed and hybridize the next generation of your plants. You can choose two plants of the same species with desirable attributes like hardiness or the production of plentiful flowers and combine them into a new plant. To perform basic crossbreeding between two of your plants, you will need to do the following procedures:

1. Choose which of the two plants will be male and which will be female. Most flowering plants can self-pollinate, which means that they have both male and female parts.
2. In the plant you've designated as the female, remove the stamens, the pollen-producing parts of the plant. You can recognize the stamens as the yellow, powdery nodes in a flower.
3. Gather the pollen—the yellow, powdery substance in the stamens—from the plant you designated as male using a Q-tip or cotton ball.
4. Apply the pollen to the pistil of the plant designated as female. The pistil is the "stalk" at the center of the flower. At the top of the pistil is the stigma, typically a sticky, bulb-shaped object meant to catch the pollen for fertilization. This is where you should apply the pollen you've taken from the male plant.
5. Cover the pistil with a transparent plastic bag to prevent pollination from other sources.
6. Wait for the fertilized flower to grow into a fruit. The harvested fruit will contain the hybridized seed.

There is an element of randomness in sexual propagation, which is why it is more challenging than asexual propagation. There is no certainty that you will get the exact desired characteristics from both plants in the resulting hybrid.

Collecting and Growing Rare Varieties

Once you've managed to propagate your houseplants for several seasons, you might start thinking about purchasing rare varieties and growing them in your own home, perhaps even selling the seeds and seedlings of these exotic and desirable plants to other plant enthusiasts. While this is certainly possible in certain circumstances, for most indoor gardeners it is not realistic to propagate rare species for commercial purposes. Unique and in-demand plants are rare often for very good reasons. For example, the fiddle leaf fig tree—considered as the "it" plant by interior designers of the last decade—is rare because it is quite a demanding plant to grow and maintain (Heath, 2022). A rare species like the infamous Shenzhen Nongke Orchid is the product of decades of cross-breeding and hybridization, "designed" to bloom only once every five years. It is far more important that you propagate and grow exotic flora that you want to collect, rather than for turning a profit. Greenhouses and plant nurseries are simply better equipped and more experienced at propagating rare plants for commercial use. Instead, grow and propagate unique species that you find compelling, interesting, and beautiful. Being able to usher in new generations of a rare plant that gives you joy is a far more fulfilling experience in your gardening journey.

6

ORCHID CARE DEMYSTIFIED

The Chinese philosopher Confucius remarked after seeing wild orchids growing in the forest: "The orchids' fragrance should be enjoyed by royalties in their residence, but they now look so solitary amongst grasses in the wild" (Poon, 2008). This is one of the earliest recorded references to orchids not only being cultivated by humans but also being traditionally grown indoors in the homes of royalty in Chinese society. Historians believe that orchid cultivation began in China or Japan about 3,000 years ago, either for medicinal or aesthetic purposes. Orchids played a key role in the European obsession with gardening during the eighteenth century, as orchid varieties brought home from the New World fascinated the Western world. Today, orchids continue to captivate and allure gardeners the world over, with their incredible variety of colors, shapes, textures, and fragrances.

While everybody loves orchids, they do have a reputation for being difficult to grow and maintain. This is largely a misconception, given that there are so many species that belong to the family Orchidaceae—an estimated 30,000 wild varieties and many more human-bred hybrids. There are thousands of individual orchid types that are easy to cultivate in your home (Frowine, 2022). One of the main reasons that orchids have such a reputation for being challenging plants is that for many years, the commercial orchid-growing industry has largely kept orchid care and maintenance practices secret. Just like any other plant, orchids require the same basic needs of light, water, temperature, and proper nutrients to survive and thrive. When coupled with key decisions that account for the conditions in your home, you too can have the immense pleasure of successfully growing orchids indoors.

Understanding Orchid Types

Popular Orchid Varieties

For anyone just starting and trying to grow orchids indoors for the first time, you can't go wrong with choosing one of the popular orchid varieties. These orchids are all easy to tend to, as their popularity has led to the cultivation and breeding of hybrids that are hardy enough to thrive in a variety of environmental conditions. Popular orchid varieties also tend to be cheap, as they are readily available in most reputable garden stores and greenhouses. You also won't be left wanting choices when it comes to these popular species, as they always have varieties that have the colors, textures, and fragrances that you are looking for.

Moth Orchids (Phalaenopsis)

These are by far the most popular type of orchids, and it is easy to understand why. Moth orchids are very easy to grow, and the "standard" hybrids of this genus are readily available practically anywhere that you can purchase plants. Moth orchids, despite being beginner-friendly, are gorgeous plants. Their flowers come in a multitude of colors, including every shade of red, orange, yellow, and purple. Their leaves and foliage are also very pretty, with complex patterns rivaling many ornamental plants. Moth orchids live for a long time, so you don't need to buy new ones or propagate from your indoor garden frequently. There are many moth-orchid hybrids today that also produce wonderful fragrances. Everything alluring about orchids is present in moth orchids, all while keeping their care and cultivation easy and stress-free.

Cattleyas

Before the current popularity of moth orchids, cattleyas used to be the iconic orchid genus. Nevertheless, cattleya orchids remain very popular and are prized especially for their large flowers, very bright colors, and pleasurable fragrances. Peru's national flower, Cattleya maxima, produces blooms as large as five inches in diameter. New hybrids called "clown" orchids feature petals with mesmerizing patterns of vividly contrasting colors. Many cattleya species are fragrant, imbuing your living spaces with wonderful, soothing scents. Wild cattleyas originated in South America, which means their ideal habitat was in tropical regions. However, cattleyas have benefitted greatly from the development of modern hybrids, which can thrive in a wider range of climate conditions.

Lady's Slippers Orchids

If you want orchids that offer more interesting and unique visual textures, you'll probably want to tend to lady's slippers orchids, or slipper orchids for short. Slipper orchids feature flowers with very vibrant colors, striking patterns on the petals and leaves, and unusually shaped structural elements because of their pouch-shaped lower petal called the labellum (Frowine, 2022). They have moderate humidity requirements and thrive in North American temperatures, which means slipper orchids do not need specialized equipment to maintain ideal temperatures and humidity. Slipper orchids also have a longer blooming period compared to other orchids, with most varieties having flowers for six to eight weeks in a year.

Picking the Right Orchid for Your Space

Choosing the perfect orchids for your home is not as daunting as it might seem. The most important environmental considerations are temperature and light, with different species of orchids requiring vastly different amounts of these two basic plant needs. It is a good idea to identify the minimum and maximum temperatures in your residence throughout the day, which can be identified using a minimum-maximum thermometer. Having this information will determine if you will need heating or cooling solutions in the indoor space where you will be growing your desired orchids. Similarly, you may want to determine the light intensity in your indoor garden with a light meter, just so you know if the orchids you want to grow can succeed with exposure to natural light in your home or if you will need to install artificial lights.

All orchids require fairly high humidity, which means humidity levels at 50 percent or greater. If you live in a region with a dry climate, you will need to bolster the humidity with a humidifier. The amount of space you have available to grow your orchids can also be an important consideration. If you have plenty of room in your home, then you can grow taller varieties of orchids like cane dendrobiums and full-size cattleyas. If space is limited, there are still many compact orchid species to choose from. Finally, good air circulation is a must when it comes to orchids, so you may need to install fans or a ventilation system to maintain access to fresh air for your orchids.

Orchid Care Myths Debunked

Myth #1 – You need a greenhouse to successfully grow orchids: Many people still believe that orchids can only thrive in the hot, humid environments that only greenhouses can provide. This is untrue, as many orchid genera, like Cymbidium and Dendrobium, actually prefer cooler temperatures. The higher humidity requirements of orchids, in general, are not too extreme as well and can be provided with a humidifier tray or regular misting.

Myth #2 – Using ice cubes to water your orchids is bad for their health: This is an interesting myth because, for many years, a lot of plant experts claimed that this was true. The idea of using ice cubes to water orchids had always been popular, and in response, many plant experts pointed out that the sudden introduction of cold temperatures could shock and injure orchids. However, a study conducted by in 2017 researchers at Ohio State University and the University of Georgia proved that using ice cubes to water orchids was not harmful, and was indeed a viable irrigation method to prevent over- or under-watering (South, et al., 2017).

Myth #3 – Orchids can be over-fertilized to encourage faster and more plentiful blooming: No amount of over-fertilizing can hurry the pace of plants. Too much fertilizer in the soil is harmful to any plant, as it disrupts the chemical balance of the soil.

Myth #4 – Orchids need repotting annually: Unnecessary repotting will only stress your orchids, stunting their growth and making them vulnerable to diseases. Only repot when the soil or growth medium has broken down, which typically happens after two to three years.

Myth #5 – Exposing orchids to more light will produce more flowers: Exposing your orchids to more sunlight than they need can be dangerous, as their leaves can dry up and burn. Maintaining ideal lighting conditions is more likely to encourage flowering than overexposure to light.

Essential Orchid Care

Orchid Potting and Media

Orchids in the wild grow on trees, with their roots relatively exposed to the air to absorb rainwater and moisture. As such, it is possible to grow orchids without any growing medium at all, using hanging pots to mimic their habitat in the wild. If you will be using a potting medium, you will need one that allows for greater air circulation and drainage compared to other plant species. As such, there are materials used in the potting media of orchids that fulfill these unique requirements.

- **Tree bark (fir, pine, redwood):** Since wild orchids grow on trees, tree bark can be used in orchid potting media. Fir is the most readily available, but is also the quickest to decompose; redwood lasts a very long time, but is difficult to source and often quite pricey.
- **Coconut husk and fiber:** When the outer covering of a coconut is dried, it becomes coco husks; when these husks are cut up and processed, they become coco fiber. Both coco husks and fiber are great materials for orchid potting media since they retain a lot of moisture while still providing plenty of air circulation. When using coco husks, make sure to wash them well before using them to remove

. the residue of salt used during the husks' production. Also, note that coco fiber does not drain as efficiently as coco husks and tree bark.

- **Osmunda fiber:** A prized orchid potting material, osmunda fiber can retain enough water for the orchids while still providing good drainage, allows for plenty of air circulation, and decomposes slowly. The only drawback is that osmunda fiber is very rare and very expensive, so take any opportunity to acquire it.

Lighting and Temperature Requirements

Because there are so many types and varieties of orchids, their lighting and temperature requirements are also incredibly diverse. Ask your orchid grower or plant nursery about the specific amounts of light needed by the particular orchid you are growing, as well as the ideal day and night temperatures you want to maintain. Like all plants, the light needs of orchids can be met by both sunlight and artificial lights. Be careful, however, when relying on sunlight, and make sure that you know how much exposure your orchid needs. Usually, the type of leaves that an orchid has is an indicator of the ideal amount of sunlight it requires. Species with narrow leaves can tolerate more exposure to direct sunlight, while broad-leafed varieties are more suited to indirect light exposure. Here are some common orchid genera and the types of leaves that they usually have:

- **Moth Orchids (Phalaenopsis):** mostly broad leaves, though there are varieties with narrow leaves
- **Cattleyas:** mostly narrow leaves

- **Lady's Slippers Orchids:** mostly broad leaves
- **Boat Orchids (Cymbidium):** narrow leaves

I learned the hard way that broad-leafed varieties should not be exposed to too much direct sunlight. I was first trying my hand at growing orchids, and I started with a pink Phalaenopsis that had broad leaves that I adored for having a striking, mottled pattern. Back then, I thought that all orchids needed plenty of light and grew in relatively high temperatures, so I placed my Phalaenopsis in a south-facing window of my home, leaving it exposed to direct sunlight. Alas, my orchid's leaves burned, drying up due to overexposure to sunlight and the accompanying high temperatures. I hope my mistake helps you recognize the importance of providing only the right amount of light and maintaining the ideal temperatures for your orchids.

Watering and Feeding Orchids

Deep watering is very effective at meeting your orchids' water requirements, especially if you have chosen a good potting medium. Soaking the potting medium in water until it can hold as much water as it can and letting the excess drain mimics how orchids get their water in the wild—rainwater soaks the roots of the orchid in the trees, with all the excess water streaming down the tree and away from the orchid. Overwatering is a constant concern for orchid enthusiasts, as this often leads to root rot. Again, so long as your plant container and the potting medium allow for good drainage, flooding the orchid's roots with too much water shouldn't be a problem when using deep watering. Also, as mentioned in the "Orchid Myths Debunked" section, watering using ice cubes is an option to avoid overwatering your orchids.

Orchids require more frequent fertilizing or "feeding" but at lower amounts when compared to other plants. This is why almost all fertilizers tailored for orchids are in liquid form, as this dilutes the fertilizer. The typical N-P-K ratio for orchid fertilizer is 20-20-20, with some exotic varieties also benefitting from vitamin and mineral amendments. Also, check that the source of nitrogen (N) in the fertilizer you are using is indicated as either "nitrate nitrogen" or "ammoniacal nitrogen," not "urea." Nitrogen provided by nitrate and ammonia are better suited for your orchids, as opposed to fertilizers that derive nitrogen from urea.

Orchid Troubleshooting and Maintenance

Orchid Pests and Diseases

Orchids are susceptible to the same common houseplant pests that we've covered in Chapter 4. Scales and spider mites are especially prevalent piercing and sucking pests that drain plant sap from orchids, causing injury and, when left unchecked, even the death of your plant. The same pest control methods apply to orchids with regard to these pests: physically removing the infested sections of your orchids, scrubbing off colonies, and using either organic or chemical pesticides. Do watch out for mice and cockroaches, as these pests have been known to feed on the leaves and flowers of orchids. Also, if you open windows or doors to allow for air circulation among your orchids, caterpillars, snails, and slugs may gain access to your indoor garden, and they are drawn to the nutrient-rich leaves of orchids.

Several houseplant diseases are also known to infect orchids. Root rot is the most common problem, which, as we've discussed, is most likely a consequence of overwatering. Fungal diseases like black rot and gray leaf spot diseases are another class of illnesses that orchids are prone to contracting. Fungi are natural competitors to orchids in the wild, as they both share a similar habitat of trees and tree bark. Stopping moisture from pooling in the parts of your orchids above the potting medium goes a long way toward protecting them from fungal diseases. Finally, a viral infection known as the mosaic virus disease is fairly common among orchids. Unfortunately, as with most viral pathogens, there is no real cure or treatment—you will have to discard the infected orchid to prevent the disease from spreading to your other houseplants. The primary symptom of the mosaic virus is the appearance of black spots that form a mottled, mosaic-like pattern on the underside of the older leaves located near the bottom of your orchids. During your weekly or monthly checkup of your plants, make sure to examine the underside of your orchids' leaves to recognize the presence of the mosaic virus.

Repotting Orchids

Repotting your orchids is essential to maintaining good drainage, ample air circulation for the roots, and providing more space for their root systems to develop. The many variables that influence your orchids' growth mean that it is not advisable to follow a "schedule" when it comes to repotting. Rather, you should examine each plant and look for signs that it is time for repotting:

- Poor drainage that results in the potting medium retaining too much water.
- The roots are overflowing or showing up on the surface of the potting medium.
- The orchid's stems, leaves, and flowers are growing beyond the edges of its container.

When you have determined that an orchid needs repotting, it is best to do so during the dormancy stage, which occurs right after the orchid has finished blooming. At this growth stage, the orchid's cells are regenerating to prepare for regrowth, making the plant more resilient to the stresses introduced by repotting. Follow this procedure to safely and effectively repot your orchids:

1. Carefully remove the orchid from its plant container, using a knife with a thin, flexible blade to loosen the roots at the edges of the container.
2. Remove any potting material that is rotten or very loose from the orchid's roots.
3. Inspect the roots and cut off any dead or decaying sections.
4. Once the only remaining roots are healthy, transfer the orchid to a new container that is one size larger than the old container. Make sure that the orchid is planted at the same depth as it was in the previous container.
5. Add fresh potting media into the new container, pressing on it to ensure that it covers the roots. Do this until the orchid is securely and firmly in place.
6. Insert a stick or stake into the potting media, then tie the leads (the tallest, most upright stems of your orchid) to the support with gardening twist ties or string.

Orchid Bloom and Growth Cycle

Understanding the growth cycle of orchids is very useful among gardeners, as many orchid care tasks like repotting, fertilizing, and pruning are best done during specific growth stages. Orchids, despite having eye-catching flowers, are perennials—this means they live for a long time, produce flowers once a year in temperate regions, then enter into a dormant state after the blooming period.

Because orchids are flowering plants, they produce seeds via self-pollination that occurs in a sexual structure unique to orchids called a column. The column contains the fused male and female parts of the flower, and orchids are the only plant species to have this specialized reproductive structure. The typical growth cycle of an orchid is as follows:

1. Seed germination – as with all plants that propagate using seeds, the orchid seed germinates to become a seedling.
2. Keiki development – some orchids, like phalaenopsis and dendrobium varieties, can also propagate asexually by growing a "keiki" from their stems. A keiki is essentially a young clone of the orchid. Keiki do not need to germinate and can be cut off and planted to become a new orchid plant.
3. Root growth – orchids are epiphytic, which means they rely on other plants or objects to provide the structure from which they will grow. Orchid roots are exposed in the wild to absorb water and nutrients from the air. As the orchid expands its root system, there will be growths known as pseudobulbs from which new leaves will emerge.
4. Leaf growth – it takes about a year for the pseudobulbs to produce leaves. Orchid leaves typically reach maturity between four to eight months.
5. Flower spike growth – once the leaves have grown fully, the flower spike will emerge. The flower spike looks like a stem, but after about three months, the flower will bloom from its tip.
6. Blooming – the blooming period of an orchid depends on the species, with some producing flowers only for a few weeks, while others will bloom for a couple of months.

7. Dormancy – after the blooming stage, the flowers will fall off and some of the older leaves will also wilt and die. The orchid is entering its dormant state. This is a great time for pruning to stimulate growth, especially at the stem so that next year's bloom will be denser and more plentiful. Continue to provide for your orchid's needs during the dormant stage.

7

GREENING YOUR INDOOR SPACE

Mark D. Sikes is one of the most prolific interior designers working in America today, working for clients like Reese Witherspoon and Nancy Meyers. In February 2022, Sikes was chosen by First Lady Jill Biden to renovate and redesign her East Wing Office at the White House. Sikes is a lover of plants and gardens: "Gardens are a passion of mine—I love the endless colors, textures, and tones of plants and flowers" (Sikes, Leffel, & Neunsinger, 2016). As such, he constantly incorporates houseplants in his various designs, recognizing how greenery naturally lends itself to being a gorgeous home décor. Using your houseplants to beautify your home is the most fun aspect of indoor gardening. Why not imbue the sterile interiors of your bathroom with lush greenery like Boston ferns, English ivy, and ZZ plants, or showcase unique and interesting plants on the bookshelves of your office or study room? In this chapter, we will explore different design philosophies and setups to decorate your home with your house-plants. The ideas to be introduced in this chapter are not meant to be prescriptions on best practices, however. The joy of decorating your home with greenery is that your approach reflects your tastes and preferences. The goal is for your home to become the embodi ment of the wonderful, beautiful you.

Plant Placement and Styling

Incorporating Houseplants into Home Décor

The main difference between your houseplants and home décor is that plants are, of course, living things, which means they have needs that must be fulfilled to remain healthy and productive. You may decide to treat your houseplants exclusively as ornamentation, placing them in ways that you find the most visually appealing.

However, if your houseplants get sick, refuse to bloom, or die, then they won't be able to beautify your home. The best way to incorporate houseplants into your home décor while still keeping them happy and healthy is to identify what plants are viable to grow in the different areas of your home. You can accomplish this easily and efficiently by following this procedure:

1. Create a table with three columns in your gardening journal, computer, or phone. For the topmost row, use the following labels—in the leftmost column, indicate "room," in the middle column, indicate "environment," and in the rightmost column, indicate "plants."

2. Go to one of the rooms you want to decorate with houseplants. Write down the name of the room as the first entry under the "room" column.

3. Examine the room for the three important environmental factors that affect plant growth and health—lighting, temperature, and humidity. Note the availability of natural and/or artificial light. Take the temperature of the room during the hottest and coolest times of the day. Determine the humidity levels of the room. Take a note of your findings as an entry under the "environment" column.

4. Repeat this assessment for all the other rooms you want to decorate with plants, writing down a new entry for every new room you examine.

5. Consult with your local greenhouse or plant nursery regarding which plants are best suited for the conditions in a given room. You may also conduct research online by using the lighting availability, minimum and maximum temperature, and humidity levels for each of the rooms as search terms.

6. List all the viable plants as an entry under the "plants" column. Repeat this for all the other rooms you've included in the table.

Having this simple table with you will be very useful, especially in between seasons, as you choose new annuals to grow or to include new plants in your indoor garden. Having the knowledge of which options are available to you for each room will keep you from being overwhelmed by too many choices, while also giving you insight as to how you would want to style your plants. Even if you do want a particular plant species in a room that does not have the ideal environmental conditions, the table will still help identify which plant necessities you will have to provide for the plant to survive.

Maximizing the Aesthetic Impact

The key to creating compelling and memorable green spaces within your home is playing around with the central elements of visual design. In all visual media and art, the central elements are color, texture, mass/volume, and proportion/scale (Kleiner, 2020). Experimenting with each of these elements—trying out different styles, combinations, and variances—will allow you to discover designs that fit your needs or align with the theme or motif you are looking for.

Color

Playing around with different color combinations is a fantastic way to come up with a design that incorporates your flowering plants. There are two main approaches you can take in terms of utilizing color for decorating your home with houseplants. First, using complementary colors allows you to make the individual hues and shades of your plants "pop" and appear more vibrant.

Complementary colors are color pairs located opposite each other in the color wheel, such as red and green or yellow and purple. These pairings make the two colors appear brighter and more intense when seen together. If you have a room in your home that is primarily blue, placing some kalanchoes or flowering maples with their orange flowers will result in a very striking color scheme. Second, you may opt to use plants with varying light and dark hues of the same color to create a unified but still interesting color scheme. This is great for organizing your ornamental plants, keeping them visually distinct while retaining a lush look. Decorating a corner of a room with light green spider plants, medium green philodendrons, and dark green snake plants will evoke that topical atmosphere and keep the colors varied.

Texture

Contrasts in visual texture are a very common and effective approach to decorating with houseplants. In spaces of your residence dominated by angular forms and smooth textures, use plants with rough, organic textures to generate visual variety. For example, in rooms with a lot of electronics like TVs and sound systems that have sleek, angular shapes, contrast can be provided by the wavy-edged leaves of the Alocasia "Polly" and the organic visual textures produced by the Monstera deliciosa's split leaves. Living walls naturally create textural contrast with the straight, rigid framing and the soft, messy tangle of the vines growing within the frame.

Mass/Volume

As with textures, contrasts in visual mass/volume make the elements of a given space more impactful. If your dining room is dominated by a heavy and robust dining table, consider using plants with lighter, more slender forms as decoration, such as the bromeliads and peace lilies. The contrasts in visual weight can also be employed among your houseplants. If you have plants with wide, broad leaves such as calatheas or elephant ears, it might be a good idea to create visual balance by placing plants with thinner, wispier structures beside them, such as English ivy or needlepoint ivy.

Proportion/Scale

Keeping relative proportions consistent when organizing your houseplants and home décor is generally a good idea. Having plants share space with home décor that is significantly larger and vice versa will diminish the aesthetic impact of the smaller ornament. This design principle is especially important when pairing plants with their containers. Growing your cute African violets in a massive vase will de-emphasize the dainty flowers as the container competes for your guests' attention. If you do end up locating small houseplants alongside large home décor, using more of the smaller greenery should keep the visuals balanced in a given space.

Feng Shui and Houseplants

Feng shui is a holistic approach to creating harmonious interactions between human beings and their environments (Kennedy, 2019). This ancient Chinese tradition has developed through millennia to find application in contemporary settings. A key concept in feng shui is the chi, the universal force or energy that flows through all living things and the natural environment. When there is a proper flow of chi in an area, individuals can enjoy the benefits of increased health, well-being, and even prosperity. Plants are very useful in feng shui, as healthy and vigorous greenery always increases chi in a given space (Barrett & Coolidge, 2003). Here are some indoor gardening pointers that coincide with the principles of feng shui:

- The best types of plants to increase the energy flowing through an area are upward-growing varieties that have round leaves. Make sure that your houseplants are healthy, as plants with drooping or wilted leaves become detrimental rather than beneficial to chi flow.
- Use plants to "soften" the energy flow in areas with sharp corners. Corners make chi flow stagnate, which reduces the natural harmony of your home. Locating plants in corners restores energy flow and invigorates the space.
- Situate plants in long hallways. Long, barren hallways make the chi flow too quickly, making them stressful and anxious spaces in your residence. Plants slow down the energy flow in these areas, which is great for producing a calmer, restorative place in your home.
- Ensure good irrigation and drainage for your plants to avoid the accumulation of stagnant water. Stagnant and dirty water generates negative chi, which can create confusion and unnecessary life entanglements.

Greening Difficult Spaces

Plants for Low-Light Areas

The primary challenge for most indoor gardeners is access to plentiful natural light. The reason why many of the most exciting varieties of flowering annuals are not grown indoors is because these species are typically summer plants, and require full sun to thrive and bloom. Unless you have the space and the resources to provide artificial light, many of the areas in your home are simply inaccessible to full sun exposure. Fortunately, there are many ornamental plants and even flowering varieties that are well-suited for low-lighting conditions. Do note that no plant can survive in complete darkness, so for spaces in your residence with particularly poor access to light, you must provide artificial lighting if you want to decorate them with greenery.

Some great ornamental plant options for low-light areas are:

- African milk tree
- Heartleaf philodendron
- Money tree
- Variegated red edge peperomia
- Watermelon begonia
- Wax begonia

These flowering varieties feature bright, vibrant colors while still being able to bloom in low-light conditions:

- African violets
- Bromeliads
- Clivia
- Gloxinia
- Moth orchids (Phalaenopsis)

Air-Purifying Plants for Allergen Control

If you or someone in your home suffers from allergies, growing particular plant species may become a problem. Most flowering plants produce pollen as part of their life cycle and propagation, which in turn may instigate an allergic reaction. Ask your physician about which plants are likely to cause allergies depending on your medical condition. That said, not all plants are detrimental to people with allergies. There are several indoor plants you can grow to help protect you and your loved ones from allergens and harmful chemicals that may be present in the air. These air-purifying plants are great if you live in dense, urban areas or locations near industrial zones.

Areca Palm: This plant is famous for its air-purifying capabilities, able to remove formaldehyde, xylene, carbon monoxide, and toluene from the air. The areca palm is also able to transpire—release moisture from its leaves—up to 1 liter of water every day, making it function as a natural humidifier. This is great for people suffering from asthma, especially during the dry winter season.

Fortune Plant (Dracaena fragrans): Dracaena is another plant known for filtering toxins. The fortune plant is especially effective in removing chemicals released from many household products, such as benzene, formaldehyde, xylene, and trichloroethylene, from the air.

Spider Plant: Besides being low-maintenance ornamental plants, spider plants are particularly good at filtering out formaldehyde in indoor spaces. Formaldehyde is found in many common household products such as detergents and other cleaning products. As such, most homes accumulate harmful formaldehyde, especially for people with allergies or asthma.

Vertical Gardening and Hanging Gardens

Having limited floor space in your residence shouldn't be a barrier to decorating your home with greenery. Vertical gardening has become a popular option for many people, especially for those living in urban areas where space is at a premium. Vertical gardening involves growing plants in tiered structures and setups, keeping the footprint of the garden very small. Many of the commercially available vertical gardening systems already incorporate irrigation and LED lighting, making them quite easy to install. These systems tend to be quite expensive, but they can be the option for you if space is constrained and you are willing to invest. Simpler, cheaper setups include creating your wall shelves where you can place your plant pots or cups or crafting a DIY living wall container.

You may also opt to utilize hanging pots or baskets for your indoor garden if space is limited. Many plants, such as orchids, actually grow in conditions similar to those of hanging containers in the wild. Plants that look great in hanging setups are those that spill out of their container, as they create interesting visual textures in your indoor spaces. Some plants you might consider for your hanging garden are:

- Cymbidium orchids
- Grape ivy
- Hoya linearis
- String of beads
- String of hearts
- Tradescantia

Themed Indoor Gardens

Succulent and Cacti Gardens

Themed indoor gardens are great for creating a unified aesthetic in decorating your home with houseplants. If you want your themed garden to be different from the typical indoor garden that features flowering and ornamental plants, you may want to opt for succulent and cacti gardens instead. Succulents and cacti offer a great variety of species to choose from. Many cacti grow beautiful and colorful flowers that rival flowering annuals and the unique forms and visual textures provided by succulents make them interesting and compelling specimens for your guests. Furthermore, cacti and succulents are low-maintenance, hardy plants, allowing for versatility in placement and decoration. Here are a few succulent and cactus species that will help you get started:

- Christmas cactus, barrel cactus, and Easter cactus all produce flowers with bright, vibrant colors.
- African milk tree, ocotillo plant, and foxtail agave are tall species that make for great centerpieces for your succulent and cacti garden.
- Bunny ears cactus, burro's tail, and moon cactus have unique, eye-catching shapes and colors.

Tropical Paradise Indoors

Another option for a themed garden is to go for a collection consisting exclusively of tropical plants. Tropical plants tend to feature bright colors and impressive foliage and will give your home an exotic, wild atmosphere. Do note that if you live in a temperate region, growing a tropical indoor garden will be a more demanding endeavor, as tropical plants have higher light, temperature, and humidity requirements. As such, it may be a good idea to locate your tropical garden in a room that has the necessary lighting and climate control systems to provide the ideal conditions for your plants. At the very least, you will need a humidifier to provide enough moisture for your tropical garden, and ideally, you would situate the plants in a south-facing window to allow for plenty of natural light. The following are fantastic tropical plants you can grow to enliven your home:

- Kentia palms, umbrella plants, and yuccas have impressive foliage that evokes the thick and lush jungle environment.
- Birds of paradise, butterfly plants, and red corals feature colorful flowers and leaves to complement your home décor.
- Hindu rope, monkey jars, and the pink quill plant have unique and interesting structures to showcase in your indoor tropical garden.

Herb and Edible Indoor Gardens

While it is true that most vegetables require a lot of sunlight to thrive, it is possible to grow edible plants indoors. The easiest option is to create your own herb garden. The most popular herbs are hardy enough to be grown in your kitchen. You will always have fresh herbs ready to use for your favorite recipes. Furthermore, you get to enjoy the wonderful fragrances of herbs, giving your home a relaxing ambiance. Some of the herbs you might consider growing are:

- Basil
- Chives
- Cilantro
- Oregano
- Thyme

You can also grow proper vegetables indoors, though this will require a decent amount of space as most vegetables develop large and deep root systems. Also, to be productive, you may need to install an LED light setup to ensure that your vegetables are getting all the light they need. This is especially important for leafy greens. Vegetables that thrive indoors are:

- Cucumber
- Garlic
- Many lettuce varieties
- Peppers
- Radishes

8

SUSTAINABILITY AND ECO-FRIENDLY HOUSEPLANT CARE

The period from 2010 to 2019 has been the hottest decade in recorded history, resulting in wildfires, hurricanes, droughts, floods, and other climate disasters devastating communities around the world (United Nations, 2023). The United Nations set goals with the Paris Agreement to reduce carbon emissions and prevent further increase of global temperatures by 1.5 degrees Celsius to avert the impending climate crisis. Now, more than ever, it is important that we pursue green initiatives to prevent further damage to the environment. It is nature that has given us the beauty and bounty of the plants we grow in our garden, and it is only right that we strive to love, care, and respect nature in return. Unfortunately, many of the established practices in gardening are unsustainable: Most commercial fertilizers are manufactured using petroleum products and other non-renewable resources, many irrigation systems utilize wasteful amounts of water and pollute water sources, and rare, exotic plants sold in developed countries are typically acquired by destroying jungles and rainforests. It is crucial that we as gardeners move away from these ecologically harmful, unsustainable practices so that we continue to receive Mother Earth's generous gifts and ensure that future generations can experience the wonders of nature.

Sustainable Gardening Practices

Reducing Plastic Use

As is the case in many industries, plastic is a ubiquitous material in gardening—many plant containers are made of plastic, and most gardening tools will have some plastic components, and the packaging of the fertilizers, garden soil, and even seeds will be made of plastic. Plastic is both cheap and versatile, which is why it is used in so many aspects of gardening. However, plastic is non-biodegradable, and many types of plastic release toxic chemicals when disposed of or discarded. Fortunately, there are many ways we can reduce our use of plastic and minimize the negative impacts of plastic waste on the environment.

- Use plant containers made up of materials other than plastic. Terracotta pots, wood trays, and metal containers are cheaper options and are also often more durable than plastic containers. Biodegradable options like baskets and cloth bags are also great alternatives for use on your annuals that will only grow for a season.
- If you are going to use plastic containers, avoid plastics made out of the polymer polyvinyl chloride (PVC). PVC is toxic to many living organisms. Check the resin identification number included in all plastic containers and avoid those designated with the numbers 1, 3, 6, and 7, as these are plastics made out of PVC.
- Try to purchase second-hand gardening tools without any plastic components. Most gardening tools are durable enough that they remain effective for decades, and it is more eco-friendly to acquire second-hand tools rather than buy new ones.
- Choose brands of fertilizers, soil, and seeds that utilize non-plastic packaging. The good news is that many companies producing these gardening products are switching to biodegradable packaging like paper and cloth. These products may be slightly more expensive than those using plastic packaging, but supporting these companies will ensure that biodegradable packaging costs will continue to go down and facilitate the complete removal of plastic packaging in gardening supplies.

Composting and Eco-Friendly Soil

All gardeners should be composting if they have the opportunity to do so, as it is the ultimate green gardening practice. Composting provides your plants with a renewable source of nutrients. It also reduces the waste produced by a household, as vegetative foodstuffs are transformed into rich fertilizers. If you are growing your own vegetables, composting essentially creates a sustainable cycle of food production for your family, significantly lessening your reliance on industrial agriculture. Unfortunately, not everyone can do composting at home. The primary limitation will be space, as you need a fairly large outdoor area to locate your compost pit. Composting is also a very laborious process, which might not fit everyone's lifestyle. Most of the so-called "compost machines" are just air-dryers, and will not produce usable compost on their own. Despite the many limitations of composting, you should still do it if you have the space and the means.

Using eco-friendly soil in your indoor garden means avoiding the use of potting soil that contains materials that are harmful to the environment. As we've discussed in Chapter 2, peat

may be prized for its high nutritional content, amazing water retention, and good air circulation, but the harvesting of peat from bogs has a massive carbon footprint. It is better to use renewable alternatives such as coco coir, which also tends to be cheaper than potting soils that use peat as a key ingredient. You must also be mindful when disposing of old soil from your indoor garden. It is generally not advisable to reuse old soil, as pests and diseases may infest and infect your new plants. Old soil is a great addition to your compost pile, with the decaying process killing off many of the harmful fungi and bacteria in the old soil. If you have a fairly large amount of old potting soil that needs to be discarded, you will have to bring it to a landfill for proper disposal. Landscapers may also buy your old soil, but these companies will only do so with large amounts.

Water Conservation and Recycling

Freshwater is rapidly becoming a very scarce resource around the world. This trend is not just happening in developing countries—in many areas of the United States like California and Texas, the depletion of freshwater sources has resulted in water costs skyrocketing in the past few years (Heyman, Mayer, & Alger, 2022). Anthropogenic climate change will only exacerbate this problem as extreme weather conditions render freshwater sources unusable or inaccessible. By adopting some fairly simple practices of water conservation and recycling, we can help contribute towards addressing this important issue:

- Use deep watering twice or thrice a week. Deep watering uses water efficiently and has the added benefit of reducing the actual time spent watering your plants.
- Water your plants after noon time. This reduces the rate of evaporation, which means more water is retained by the soil for a longer period.
- Recycle water used in cooking and/or washing dishes. The water you use to boil your pasta, wash your rice, or clean your dishes does not need to go to waste. Use it instead to water your plants. Do note that if you are using dishwater, make sure that you are also using "green" or "natural" dishwashing detergents. These are biodegradable and do not contain chemicals that may harm your plants.

Responsible Plant Acquisition

Avoiding Plants From Poaching and Illegal Trade

Illegal wildlife trade has become a widespread problem globally and is now considered one of the largest criminal sectors in the world after drug trafficking, human trafficking, and counterfeit crimes (Kew Royal Botanical Gardens, 2020). One of the longest-running efforts to curtail illegal wildlife trade has been the Convention on the International Trade in Endangered Species of Wild Fauna and Flora (CITES), a regulatory framework first enforced in 1975. To avoid purchasing plants via illegal trade, it is a good idea to check if the species you want to buy is listed as an endangered species under CITES regulations. You can visit the website Species+ (https://www.speciesplus.net/) to search the CITES databases. If you discover that the species is endangered, then any sellers offering that plant for purchase are engaging in illegal trade. Orchids, cycads, and cacti are the most commonly poached plants sold in illegal markets.

Supporting Ethical Growers and Sellers

We must support growers and sellers who employ ethical and sustainable practices in sourcing and cultivating the plants they make available for purchase. This will encourage improvement across the entire industry so that we can be sure that growers and sellers are enacting green initiatives and are not using exploitative measures that harm ecosystems and communities around the world. Unfortunately, there are currently no regulatory bodies in most developed countries that ensure ethical and sustainable prac- tices are being used by plant growers and sellers. We need to be careful when a plant vendor makes claims about sustainable sourcing of their offerings, as the pathways of acquiring plants—especially rare and exotic ones—are publicly not transparent. The best way to know if a grower or seller is worth supporting is by observing their practices firsthand. Some things you want to look out for are:

- Is the vendor willing to identify where they source their plants? Growers and sellers who are transparent about where they get their stock are more likely to employ ethical standards in sourcing plants.
- Does the vendor have extensive knowledge of their offerings? A good grower and seller should be able to tell you the natural habitat of a plant, any special requirements the plant may need, and the expected characteristics of the plant in each of its developmental stages.
- Are the vendor's prices competitive with the current market? If the plants being sold are too cheap, there is a good chance that they were grown unsustainably or acquired through unethical means. If the prices are too high, the vendor might be exploiting demand by placing too high of a markup.

Saving Threatened Species Through Cultivation

It is estimated that one out of five plant species are currently facing the threat of extinction (Waddington, 2021). Part of the conservation efforts being taken by organizations around the world is having home gardeners cultivate endangered plant species. In the U.S., the Center for Plant Conservation (CPC) is responsible for protecting these threatened species. The CPC website has a Rare Plant Finder (https://saveplants.org/rare-plants-near-me/) that you can use to identify rare plants in your region that you can try to cultivate at home. The CPC website also provides resources and guides to help you grow these rare and endangered species. Besides the CPC, many universities also have conservation programs that allow home gardeners to cultivate endangered plants. Enquire about these programs in the botany or biology departments of universities in your area.

Indoor Ecosystems

Terrariums and Miniature Ecosystems

Terrariums are an eco-friendly way to grow your plants, as a good terrarium setup aims to create a miniature ecosystem that is self-sustaining—it consumes little to no additional resources and requires minimal maintenance. While you could make a large, elaborate terrarium consisting of many different plants and animals, it is very easy to create one contained in a cookie or mason jar. A basic terrarium has the following components:

- A drainage layer where excess water will settle. This layer is composed of small rocks or pebbles.
- A growth medium where the plants will grow. A standard potting mix should be suitable for this top layer, although it is a good idea to supplement it with additional nutrients by adding compost or other organic fertilizing material like chicken or worm castings.
- Moss to cover and provide structure to the growth medium. Cushion moss and fern moss are excellent choices.
- Plants that thrive in partial sun to full shade. It is not ideal to place your terrarium in direct sunlight as this will dry up

the moss, so plants that grow well in dimmer lighting conditions are your best options.

- Scavenger organisms that will eat decaying matter and harmful fungi. Pill bugs, pond snails, and springtails are great scavengers whose excrement will also provide nutrients for your plants.

Native Plants in Your Home

Native plants are species that have evolved to grow well in the environmental conditions of a specific region. Natives are differentiated from cultivars, which are species and varieties that have been bred by humans to manifest desirable characteristics such as more variety in colors for the flowers or leaves, or more bountiful produce. Though native plants are "wild," they will be easier to tend to and maintain if you choose natives that grow locally in your region. After all, the light, humidity, and temperature where you live are at the exact levels for the local native plant to thrive. Choosing to grow natives in your home helps maintain the health of the local ecosystem, as these species already have key roles to play in the natural biological processes that sustain said ecosystem. Native flowers provide food to local pollinating insects, and woody perennials are typically habitat for all manner of birds and small mammals. You might even want to devote a space within your residence to exclusively grow native plants, as a way to showcase and celebrate the local flora in your region.

Building a Balanced Indoor Biodiversity

It can be tempting to have your indoor garden comprised of plants with similar needs, both for practical and aesthetic reasons. It is definitely easier for you as a gardener to grow only low-maintenance plants with the same lighting, temperature, and humidity requirements, and it is impressive to showcase your collection of cattleyas in full bloom. A lack of biodiversity in your indoor garden, however, introduces several issues. Having similar species make up the majority of your household plants makes pests and diseases more dangerous, as one type of infestation or infection can easily decimate all of your greenery. Moreover, growing similar plants can end up consuming more resources in the long term, as they degrade soil quality at a faster rate. An indoor garden with a more balanced, biodiverse set of plants will be more resilient to a wider range of pests and diseases. Also, you can practice crop rotation to allow some plants to help regenerate soil health. Having more species and varieties of plants also "spaces out" the peak seasons throughout the year, so that the same plant maintenance tasks like pruning or repotting are not concentrated at similar periods. For example, it can be overwhelming to try to finish all the end-of-summer tasks if you only grow annuals. A balanced garden distributes plant mainte-nance tasks more evenly throughout the year, ultimately making plant care easier.

9

YOUR FLOURISHING INDOOR GARDEN

Congratulations! We've covered a plethora of topics throughout this book that should provide you with the knowledge to grow a lush, beautiful, and thriving indoor garden. Creating a green haven in your own home is cause for celebration, but this is also a time for reflection on what your garden means to you. A major part of gardening alongside cultivating your plants is cultivating your growth as a person. Wonderfully, our houseplants contribute to our self-cultivation, providing emotional support, improving our mental health and well-being, and complementing our personalities and identities. Up to this point, we have primarily focused on gardening as a solitary activity—we learned how to tend to the plants we chose, we discovered how to beautify our homes with our plants using our style, and we recognized how our indoor garden can become an expression of ourselves. Ultimately, however, the gardening journey is best shared with others. Our love for plants provides a strong foundation for the creation of a dedicated and passionate community along with other gardeners. Moreover, we can give our family and friends one of life's greatest gifts, which is to share with them our passion for greenery. What better way to celebrate our growth as gardeners than to inspire someone to come along with us on our journey?

Creating a Personal Garden Sanctuary

The Emotional Connection to Your Plants

While it is true that plants are neither sentient nor self-aware, we gardeners still cultivate an intimate, emotional connection with our plants. As we've discussed in Chapter 7 when we covered feng shui, plants both generate and channel life energy in your home. As such, we must strengthen our connection with our green companions by giving them our life energy through expressions of positive, life-affirming emotions.

When tending to your houseplants, make sure that you are in a happy mood, as your greenery will absorb and channel that emotional energy. Talk to your plants, and even sing to them—we know from various studies that plants respond to auditory stimuli. Feel your plants' roots, stems, and leaves when taking care of their needs, to convey to them your appreciation and affection. You will feel your emotional connection with your plants growing as your home becomes imbued with an atmosphere of joy and love.

Mindfulness and Well-Being Through Gardening

The therapeutic effects of gardening on mental health and well-being are well documented, with a recent 2022 study finding that people who engaged in gardening experienced reduced symptoms of depression and anxiety, while also improving the individual's mood in daily activities, quality of life, and general mindfulness (Yang, et al., 2022). While tending to your indoor garden already gives you respite from the stresses and anxieties of everyday life, there are many other activities that you can combine with gardening to improve your mental health.

- Your indoor garden is a fantastic place for meditation. Plants give off oxygen, making an indoor garden a naturally soothing space.
- Create a painting or illustration in your indoor garden. Art therapy does wonders for a person's mental health, and you can even have your houseplants as the subjects of your artwork.

- Write your gardening journal among your houseplants. A gardening journal is very useful in planning out your indoor garden, and it also gives you time to mindfully focus and reflect on your gardening journey.

Houseplants as an Extension of Self

As you become a more experienced gardener, you will find that your garden becomes a reflection of who you are. After all, the plants you choose to grow are based on your preferences, and it is very easy to see one's self in plants, as there is the same diversity and uniqueness among flora that can be found among individual human beings. Perhaps the hardy snake plant or Chinese evergreen appeals to you because you exhibit the same tenacity, or maybe you appreciate the simple but elegant beauty of tulips as the flowers mirror your personality. Embrace the fact that your houseplants end up becoming an extension of yourself. Be proud of the green haven you've created, just as you are proud of your amazing, one-of-a-kind identity.

Sharing the Love

Passing on Your Knowledge

Gardening is too beautiful an experience for it not to be shared with others. It doesn't matter if you are a beginning or veteran gardener; it is always great to share whatever knowledge you have acquired with anyone interested in growing and tending to plants. The discoveries we make in each of our own unique gardening experiences can be contextualized and applied to similar situations to help others in their gardening journey. So don't be shy when a friend or family member getting into the hobby asks you questions related to gardening. Just be honest and give them an answer based on what has worked for you. A fantastic way to pass on your knowledge to your loved ones is by sharing your gardening journal with them. You can upload your gardening journal to a variety of online platforms such as blogs or record vlogs for the various entries. In this way, your knowledge can become an easily accessible resource that can aid other gardeners.

Plant Gifting and Sharing

Plants make for wonderful gifts to family and friends and can help you develop your skills in propagating and cultivating various species of flora. Do remember that plants are living things that need care, attention, and love to survive and thrive, which means that you are imparting some responsibilities towards plant care whenever you decide to gift someone with greenery. Here are some pointers to remember when gifting houseplants:

- When gifting plants to non-gardeners or people who are just beginning their gardening journey, choose low-maintenance varieties. It is also a good idea to accompany your gift with a note card that details how to take care of the plant's basic needs.
- If you are gifting a plant to someone you already know who is interested in taking up gardening as a hobby, you can accompany the plant with essential gardening tools and resources to get them started in their gardening journey. You might even choose to gift them a seedling so that they can enjoy the satisfaction and fulfillment of cultivating the plant to maturity.

- Choose a beautiful, sturdy, and practical container for the plant you are gifting. You don't want the recipient of your gift to have to repot the plant, not only for convenience but also to avoid inflicting unnecessary stress to the plant. Avoid using disposable plastic containers—a good terracotta or metal container is more environmentally friendly as it can be reused or repurposed as the recipient sees fit to their needs.

Building Community Through Houseplants

Being part of a community of plant lovers is the best way to not only share your passion with others, it also allows you to more quickly expand your knowledge and develop your skills as a gardener. There are many ways to find the gardening community that is best for you. Probably the most convenient means is by looking for gardening groups and clubs online. The recent resurgence in gardening as a hobby has made gardening groups very popular on social media, and many of them also meet face-to-face. Most greenhouses, gardening stores, and plant nurseries also have their own gardening club or group. If not, they will still know any local gardening communities you can join. Community gardens are excellent places to connect with other gardeners, while also getting to know better the members of your community. Community gardens also have the benefit of sharing resources like gardening/potting soil, compost, and fertilizer with everyone who chooses to contribute to the garden. Finally, you can opt to create your own gardening community, starting a group or club with your family, friends, and neighbors. Whichever option you decide to pursue, what is important is that you look for a friendly, loving group of people who all share in their love for plants and gardening.

Future Visions

Looking Forward to Future Houseplant Trends

Discovering the latest houseplant and gardening trends is not just about following a new "fad" on which varieties are fashionable to grow. Knowing about new cultivars can allow you to grow a species that you weren't able to before, and understanding a new technique in gardening will improve your plant care routines. A great way to remain updated on future houseplant trends is through a trusted plant grower and/or seller. They are the first ones to know about new cultivars that become commercially available and can inform you about the specific needs of the newly available plants for your home. New techniques and approaches to gardening are covered extensively by most gardening websites. It is a good idea to explore different sources when you discover a new gardening concept, as some techniques might just be part of a gardening website's marketing or were sponsored by a particular company. Once you've identified a new gardening trend, consult with your gardening supply store or greenhouse to learn more about the particular trend.

Sustainable Houseplant Care as a Way of Life

We discussed many sustainable approaches towards plant care in Chapter 8, but to adopt these practices for the long term, it is useful to treat them not as individual tasks but rather as a holistic way of life. Taking this perspective will not only make these ecologically conscious practices more effective, it will also help you recognize new sustainable practices that are specific to your situation. Once you've established sustainability as a core principle that informs your gardening style, green practices will naturally manifest in all the plant care activities that you do. For example, if you find that your indoor garden produces a lot of excess water, having a framework of sustainability will enable you to recognize that the excess water is wasteful, and so you will seek out solutions that will either minimize the excess water or reuse that water. The environmentally conscious mindset will also find its way into other aspects of your life, which is a good thing since our societies need to be more mindful of the ways that our everyday lives impact nature.

Houseplant Legacy and the Joy of Passing It On

> *And listen, my father's mother—midwife*
> *and singer of poems, that champion laugher*
> *whose fat roses scented my early days—*
> *under my nails, wherever I dig, still*
> *laughing. I tell her I sing roses too,*
> *my hands in dirt where she lives forever.*

This is the last stanza in Rhina P. Espaillat's poem "Gardening" (1994). Here, she highlights the beautiful connection that gardens create among individuals across multiple generations. Through gardening, your loved ones can look back at the wonderful memories they have shared with you. Moreover, passing on stewardship of your garden serves as a testament to your love of nature, conveying the appreciation and respect you hold towards all life in the world. In this regard, a garden passed on becomes a reminder of humanity's responsibility towards nature. Finally, passing on your garden to your loved ones gives them something that all human beings strive for - a chance to achieve true happiness. The times I have spent in my garden are some of the most joyful and fulfilling moments in my life, and I can think of no better gift to give to the people I care about the most.

MAKE A DIFFERENCE WITH YOUR REVIEW
PLANT SEEDS OF KINDNESS WITH YOUR REVIEW

"The true gardener, like a good artist, is not the one who puts the most into their work, but the one who gets the most out of it."

UNKNOWN

Did you know that people who give without expecting anything in return tend to be happier and more fulfilled? That's what we're aiming for in our journey together. And I have a special request for you...

Would you help someone you've never met, just for the joy of it?

Who is this mysterious person, you ask? They're a lot like you used to be. Eager to learn about houseplants, wanting to make their home greener, and looking for guidance, but still trying to figure out where to start.

Many people choose books based on their covers and what others say about them. So here's my request on behalf of a budding houseplant enthusiast you've never met:

Please help them by leaving a review of this book. Your review could help...

- ...one more person create a calming green space in their home.
- ...one more family enjoy the beauty of nature indoors.
- ...one more student learn about the wonders of plant care.

- ...one more green thumb discover their passion.
- ...one more dream of a lush indoor garden come true.

To spread this joy and make a difference, all you have to do is...take a moment to...

leave a review.

Just scan the QR code below to share your thoughts:

Thank you from the bottom of my heart. Now, let's get back to our green journey.

Your biggest fan, Natalia Kozlova

PS - Here's a fun fact: Sharing something valuable with someone enhances your value in their eyes. If this book will help another plant enthusiast, why not share it with them? Let's spread the love for houseplants together!

BONUS CHAPTER: PET-FRIENDLY HOUSEPLANT CARE

I f you love plants, then it is very likely that you love animals, too. As such, you may also have pets at home, which can introduce some problems for your indoor garden. Dogs and cats can chew on your houseplants' leaves and stems, dig up and disturb their root systems, or damage essential plant maintenance systems or installations you've set up. At the same time, there are several plant species and varieties that can be harmful to your pets. Some plants are poisonous to dogs, cats, or both, causing illness or even fatality when ingested, while other plants can cause a harmful reaction that can injure your pets. It is therefore crucial to adopt practices that protect both your plants and your pets from causing each other harm. To do this, we must first identify which plants are toxic to our pets, replace them with pet-safe alternatives, and encourage pet behavior that minimizes the damage they can cause to plants.

Identifying Toxic Houseplants

Common Toxic Plants: Recognizing the Culprits

There are a surprising number of plants that are toxic to cats and dogs. You can find comprehensive lists of plants toxic to pets at the official website of the American Society for the Prevention of Cruelty to Animals (ASPCA). If you are just starting an indoor garden, consider these toxic plants when choosing which species and varieties you want to grow. Here are some popular indoor plants that can be harmful to your animal companions:

Autumn Crocus – this fall-blooming annual is very popular for its vibrant color, but it can cause multi-organ damage to your pets when ingested.

Azalea/Rhododendron – these perennials produce grayantoxins which are harmful to many animals' gastrointestinal and nervous systems.

Chrysanthemums – chrysanthemums contain the chemical pyrethrin, which can upset your pets' gastrointestinal system, causing drooling, vomiting, and loss of appetite.

Lilies – lilies are very toxic to cats, as ingesting even small amounts can lead to severe kidney damage to our feline friends.

Pothos – these common trailing houseplants are a staple ornamental in temperate regions, but they can cause gastrointestinal swelling and irritation among your pets.

Lesser-Known Toxic Plants: Hidden Dangers

Unfortunately, many tropical plant species can be toxic to your animal companions. Keep this in mind when you decide to take care of rarer, more exotic plant varieties, as you will need to enact measures to prevent your pets from being poisoned. Here are some lesser-known plant species that are toxic to cats and dogs:

Bird of Paradise flower – known for its beautiful, colorful flowers that resemble tropical birds, its fruit and seeds can cause vomiting and drowsiness among your pets.

Lobelia – lobelias are popular tropical plants because of their cute, pastel-colored blooms, but they are very toxic to small mammals, causing rapid failures of their nervous and digestive systems when ingested.

Swiss cheese plant (Monstera deliciosa) – this unique-looking ornamental is also known as the "dumb cane," since it causes your pet's tongue to swell causing them to lose their voice. The irritation can become so severe that your pet might have trouble breathing and suffer choking.

Plant Poisoning Symptoms in Pets

The majority of plants toxic to your pets impact the gastrointestinal tract, hence, the most common plant poisoning symptoms involve problems with the animal's digestive system:

- Excessive drooling
- Nausea/vomiting
- Diarrhea
- Loss of appetite

There are also more subtle behavioral symptoms that you can look out for when you suspect your pets have been poisoned by plants:

- Drowsiness
- Sluggishness
- Depression

Symptoms that indicate severe poisoning and require immediate medical aid are:

- Collapse
- Convulsions/Tremors
- Difficulty breathing
- Extremely weak pulse

Poisonous Plant Alternatives

Safe Houseplants for Pet-Friendly Homes

Although many plants are toxic to our furry friends, there are still plenty of safe options for your indoor garden. Most of these pet-friendly varieties are non-flowering ornamentals, which means they are often low-maintenance, hardy species you can locate pretty much anywhere in your home. They are great in spaces where your pets frequent, such as the living room and hallways.

- African violet
- Areca palm
- Baby's tears
- Boston fern
- Calathea
- Echeveria
- Haworthia
- Orchids
- Peperomia
- Spider plant

Creating a Pet-Safe Indoor Garden

As is the case with many of the aspects of gardening, creating an indoor garden that is safe for pets involves good planning. The most ideal situation in this regard is, of course, to only grow plants that are safe for your animal companions. Admittedly, this will prevent you from growing all the varieties you would want to beautify your home. A possible option is to keep your indoor garden in a room or area that is inaccessible to your pets. This will not only prevent your pets from being poisoned, but it will also protect your plants from being damaged by your pets. One thing you do want to do is keep your pets away from your gardening supplies. Fertilizers, especially chemical ones, are dangerous to animals, and your gardening/potting soil may get contaminated or infected by pests or diseases from your pets. Housing your plants inside terrariums is another pet-safe approach to your indoor garden, although larger dogs and cats can topple over and break your glass containers, so make sure your terrariums are situated in out-of-reach, stable locations of your home.

Tips for Transitioning Toxic Plants Out

If your family is getting its first pet, you may decide to phase out all of the toxic plants from your indoor garden. Ideally, you get your pet at the end of a season when you are going to replace your annuals anyway. This will enable you to choose new annuals that pose no threat to your new animal friend. You can also replace your perennials with pet-safe species during winter when most perennials go into dormancy. If you can't wait for the end of the season or end of the year, it is best to isolate your toxic plants and render them inaccessible to your new pet, up until you can find these plants a new home by donating them to a friend or your local community garden.

Managing Indoor Pet Behavior

Curbing Plant-Chewing Habits

Unfortunately for pet-owning gardeners, cats and dogs have an instinct to chew on various objects. This becomes a problem when your pets decide to chew on your houseplants. There are many ways to train your animal friends and prevent them from damaging your indoor garden:

- Make sure that your pets are well-fed. Dogs are especially prone to chewing on inappropriate objects when they are hungry.
- Provide chewing toys to your pets to discourage chewing on your houseplants. Cats and dogs will typically favor chewing the toys they recognize that they "own" over other objects in your home.
- Use chewing deterrents to dissuade your pets from chewing inappropriate objects. Many natural sprays have undesirable tastes and smells to your pets that can be used on houseplants to prevent chewing.

Safe and Fun Pet Interaction with Plants

While there are various considerations to ensure that your plants and your pets are kept safe, healthy, and happy, this does not mean that you can't enjoy activities that involve your animal friends interacting with your indoor garden. Catnips are nontoxic plants that serve as a fun treat for your feline buddies. Herbs like cat thyme and mint are also great stimulants for cats. Similarly, many fragrant plant species are suitable for entertaining your dogs. As with humans, chamomile and lavender have a calming and relaxing effect on dogs, particularly among curious breeds that love sniffing. Barley grass is a fantastic digestive aid for canines and is very easy to grow indoors.

Preventing Accidents and Mishaps

Having active, playful pets in your home can sometimes lead to accidents and mishaps that damage your houseplants. To prevent these occurrences, it is a good idea to use sturdy and robust plant containers for your indoor garden. Your more delicate greenery should be kept out of reach of your pets, and hanging containers can be very useful in this regard. In the same way that you train your dogs or cats to avoid scratching or damaging furniture, you should also discourage them from attacking your indoor flora. Clearly identifying the objects and toys that your pets can play with should teach them not to attack your indoor garden, and will create a harmonious environment between your plant and animal companions within your home.

REFERENCES

Abdalla, S. (2023, August 31). *A brief history of indoor plants: How the Ancient Egyptians started the 5,000 year-old trend.* CSA Living. https://csa-living.org/oasis-blog/a-brief-history-of-indoor-plantsnbsphow-the-ancient-egyptians-started-the-5000-year-old-trend

Avery, R. (2022, April 26). *Celebrity chefs' stunning homes: John Torode, Gordon Ramsay, Jamie Oliver and more.* Hello! https://www.hellomagazine.com/homes/20220426138816/celebrity-chefs-houses-inside-photos/

Barrett, J., & Coolidge, J. (2003). *Feng shui your life.* Sterling Publishing Co., Inc.

Bauder, T., Wardle, E., & Waskom, R. (2020, June). *Best management practices: Agricultural pesticide use.* Colorado State University: https://extension.colostate.edu/docs/pubs/crops/xcm177.pdf

Beavers, A. W., Atkinson, A., Varvatos, L. M., Connolly, M., & Alaimo, K. (2022). How gardening in Detroit influences physical and mental health. *International Journal of Environmental Research and Public Health, 19*(13), Article 7899.

Chia, S. Y., & Lim, M. W. (2022). A critical review on the influence of humidity for plant growth forecasting. *IOP Conference Series: Materials Science and Engineering*, 1-7.

Das, M. (2023). Potential effects of audible sound signals including music on plants: A new trigger. *Environment Conservation Journal, 24*(3), 296-304.

Deike, C. (2020, June 17). *Pros & cons of different types of garden containers.* Garden Gate Magazine. https://www.gardengatemagazine.com/articles/containers/all/different-types-of-garden-containers/

Dzhambov, A. M., Lercher, P., Browning, M. H., Stoyanov, D., Petrova, N., Novakov, S., & Dimitrova, D. D. (2021). Does greenery experienced indoors and outdoors provide an escape and support mental health during the COVID-19 quarantine? *Environmental Research, 196*, Article 110420.

Earle, A. M. (2014). *Old time gardens, newly set forth: A book of the sweet o' the year.* Cambridge University Press.

Espaillat, R. P. (1994, June). Gardening. *Poetry*, p. 141.

Frowine, S. A. (2022). *Orchids for dummies, 2nd Edition.* John Wiley & Sons, Inc.

Grant, A. (2022, December 16). *Deep water culture for plants: How to build a deep water culture system.* Gardening Know How: https://www.gardeningknowhow.com/special/containers/deep-water-culture-for-plants.htm

Hansen, K. (2020, April 29). *12 stars cultivate green thumbs during the pandemic.*

Architectural Digest. https://www.architecturaldigest.com/story/celebrities-gardening-while-stuck-at-home

Heath, S. (2022, March 2). *Six of the most expensive houseplants—and why.* The Spruce. https://www.thespruce.com/most-expensive-houseplants-5080132

Heyman, J. M., Mayer, A., & Alger, J. (2022). Predictions of household water affordability under conditions of climate change, demographic growth, and fresh groundwater depletion in a southwest US city indicate increasing burdens on the poor. *PLoS One, 17*(11), e0277268.

Jellicoe, G. (1995). *Geoffrey Jellicoe: The studies of a landscape designer over 80 years.* Garden Art Press.

Johnstone, G. (2023, January 3). *6 indoor plant lighting tips to help your plants thrive.* Reader's Digest. https://www.rd.com/article/indoor-plant-lighting/

Kennedy, D. D. (2019). *Feng shui for dummies, 2nd Edition.* Wiley Publishing, Inc.

Kew Royal Botanical Gardens. (2020, October). *FloraGuard: Tackling the illegal trade in endangered plants.* Kew Royal Botanical Gardens: https://www.kew.org/sites/default/files/2020-10/FloraGuard%20Tackling%20the%20illegal%20trade%20in%20endangered%20plants.pdf

Kleiner, F. S. (2020). *Gardner's art through the ages, 16th edition.* Cengage Learning.

Leone, J. (2017, April 24). *LED lights for plant growth.* Sciencing. https://sciencing.com/the-effect-of-light-on-plant-growth-12201478.html

Lusiardi, F. (2023, July 2). *When did they get into our homes? A brief history of houseplants.* Inexhibit. https://www.inexhibit.com/case-studies/when-did-they-get-into-our-homes-a-brief-history-of-houseplants/

Morris, P. L. (2011). Bonsai moves indoors. In P. L. Morris, & S. W. Saphire (Eds.), *Growing bonsai indoors* (pp. 5-7). Brooklyn Botanic Garden, Inc.

Muth, P. F. (2011). Bonsai styles. In P. L. Morris, & S. W. Saphire (Eds.), *Growing bonsai indoors* (pp. 9-19). Brooklyn Botanic Garden, Inc.

Pollan, M. (2006). *The omnivore's dilemma: A natural history of four meals.* The Penguin Press.

Poon, A. (2008, February 6). *The orchid and Confucius.* Asia Sentinel. https://www.asiasentinel.com/p/the-orchid-and-confucius

Sideman, R. (2017, April). *Starting plants from seed [Fact Sheet].* University of New Hampshire. https://extension.unh.edu/sites/default/files/migrated_unmanaged_files/Resource000495_Rep517.pdf

Sikes, M. D., Leffel, C., & Neunsinger, A. (2016). *Beautiful: All-American decorating and timeless style.* Rizzoli International Publications, Inc.

South, K. A., Thomas, P. A., van Iersel, M. W., Young, C., & Jones, M. L. (2017). Ice cube irrigation of potted Phalaenopsis orchids in bark media does not decrease display life. *HortScience, 52*(9), 1271-1277.

Streep, P., & Glover, J. (2003). *Spiritual gardening: Creating sacred space outdoors.* Inner Ocean Publishing, Inc.

United Nations. (2023). *Sustainable development goals.* United Nations. https://www.un.org/sustainabledevelopment/climate-change/

Verey, R., Lord, T., & Wills, H. (1995). *Rosemary Verey's making of a garden.* Henry Holt and Company.

Waddington, E. (2021, August 13). *12 common container garden mistakes you might be making.* Rural Sprout. https://www.ruralsprout.com/container-garden-mistakes/

Waddington, E. (2022, January 11). *Turn your garden into a refuge for rare and endangered plants.* Treehugger. https://www.treehugger.com/safeguarding-rare-endangered-plants-garden-5214837

Yang, Y., Ro, E., Lee, T.-J., An, B.-C., Hong, K.-P., Yun, H.-J., . . . Choi, K.-H. (2022). The multi-sites trial on the effects of therapeutic gardening on mental health and well-being. *International of Environmental Research and Public Health, 19*(13), 8046-8058.

Made in United States
Troutdale, OR
11/13/2024

24732718R00086